Forgiveness

Forgiveness

BREAKING FREE AND MOVING ON

Peter Doherty
and Patti-Anne Kay

NOVALIS

© 2017 Novalis Publishing Inc.

Cover design: Martin Gould
Cover photo: iStockphoto / Pgiam
Layout: Audrey Wells

Published by Novalis

Publishing Office
10 Lower Spadina Avenue, Suite 400
Toronto, Ontario, Canada
M5V 2Z2

Head Office
4475 Frontenac Street
Montréal, Québec, Canada
H2H 2S2

www.novalis.ca

Library and Archives Canada Cataloguing in Publication
Doherty, Peter, 1957-, author
    Forgiveness / Rev. Peter Doherty, Patti-Anne Kay.
ISBN 978-2-89688-434-6 (softcover)
    1. Forgiveness. I. Kay, Patti-Anne, 1949-, author II. Title.
BF637.F67D64 2017   155.9'2   C2016-907962-7

Printed in Canada.

We acknowledge the support of the Government of Canada.

5 4 3 2 1   21   20   19   18   17

CONTENTS

INTRODUCTION

Our Journeys with Forgiveness

You may wonder, "Why another book on forgiveness? Is there anything new? I've tried to forgive, but I just can't. Do I even want to forgive?" We wanted to make our work accessible so that more people can benefit from life-changing forgiveness. We've seen men and women become free as they move towards resolution of conflict and the healing of relational wounds. We wanted to share what we've gained after working on forgiveness issues with people, young and old, from different cultures and countries, from people with no religious or spiritual connection to those of diverse spiritual and religious backgrounds.

We've seen first-hand the pain experienced by those who are blocked by misunderstanding or erroneous beliefs about forgiving. Too often we've seen people struggle with unresolved forgiveness at the end of their life. The depth of pain they suffer as a result of unresolved conflict is agonizing. We wanted to help so that no one has to struggle over unresolved forgiveness at his or her last breath.

Our work on forgiveness stems from our collaboration, based in our different backgrounds and professional training, and our respective work as a teacher, campus minister and spiritual director (Patti-Anne) and a parish priest, psychologist, and family therapist (Peter). Between us, we have worked in counselling, including marriage, spiritual and pastoral counselling, hospital chaplaincy, and with groups, offering retreats and workshops. We've found that our different training, perspectives, and experience strengthens the work. We were able to access a particular richness derived from a different way of seeing the world integrating a masculine and feminine perspective. For both of us, forgiveness has been a healing issue, in our work and in our lives.

Simply put, for us, Christ is the model not just of forgiveness, but for life. We cannot overemphasize the significance of the gift of forgiveness in Christ's life and teachings, in his words, and through his actions. For Christians, forgiveness is part of the bedrock of faith. However, we approach forgiveness from a broad stance, one that invites *everyone* to benefit by forgiving, whether they are religious or not. As an essential part of that inclusiveness, we integrate the human sciences with spirituality, and the wisdom of many religious traditions.

Forgiveness work has helped us make sense of life and live fully engaged lives. In the normal course of our work, our focus is on others, with deep listening, engaging our experience and training to help them through difficulties. When we asked a friend to read a draft of our book, he commented that he would like to know more about us, about our stories. It was a lightbulb moment that lies at the heart of what we're trying to do: not only by blending our work and professional training with others, but by integrating insights that come through our lives. This is the lived knowledge. We are thankful for that suggestion and share some of our own lived forgiveness here.

Peter

My own journey with forgiveness began over 35 years ago. I had experienced betrayals in my religious community and work that resulted in feelings of anger. Over time, the anger became buried and I thought I had moved on. I didn't realize that I was still bitter and had developed a short fuse. My sister challenged me, pointing out how my anger was poisoning our relationship. Initially, I denied her perception, but within a few days, I realized that despite all my training in psychology and spirituality, I was not in touch with my feelings. Unfortunately, being aware of the anger and painful feelings did not solve the problem, but I embarked on a journey of learning about forgiveness and how to forgive so I could move on. Much of what is presented here is part of that journey.

I learned that struggling with forgiveness has nothing to do with our intelligence or education, nor does it mean that something is wrong with us. Through research, interviews, and feedback from people who attended our workshops, and many discussions with my co-author, Patti-Anne, several themes and insights kept reappearing. The book you are reading reflects our personal journeys. We hope you will be able use our experiences as guides for your own journey.

Patti-Anne

I became more deeply in touch with forgiveness while serving as an interfaith chaplain at a large hospital. As this was in a multicultural city, the hospital staff, the doctors and nurses, as well as the patients and their families, represented a wonderful diversity. This meant I was present with a range of people with various customs and backgrounds as they journeyed to the end of life, and I also spent time with those who grieved their loss.

I learned that forgiveness issues touch everyone; this was far more than a deathbed issue. I witnessed the depth of anguish in those who were dying, and in those who mourned, and I noticed that what I called "forgiveness grief" added another dimension to their suffering. I saw that struggling with forgiveness was a common bond for people from all walks of life, from all kinds of faith backgrounds, for men and women at different stages of life, and from different cultures.

It's difficult to describe the pain felt by those who would have given anything to try and make amends, to reconcile, or, at the very least, to say they were sorry. This was also true for those mourning the loss of a loved one; they, too, experienced forgiveness grief for the lost opportunity to forgive and be forgiven.

Even though I knew about forgiveness, I didn't experience it for myself in a profound way until my mother's end-of-life journey. While it may seem blindingly obvious, it is one thing to be present with others as they struggle with forgiveness, and altogether different to be there with your own mother. This began a new journey for me, and left me with a greater desire not just to work with others on the theme of forgiveness, but to share this work with a wider audience in a book.

How This Helps You

Here you have a practical, hands-on approach that addresses your thoughts, feelings, and actions. The Tools and Strategies help you forgive in your own time and in your own way. The Tools provide concrete steps to integrate the changes you want in your life. This helps you build healthy relationships and set appropriate personal boundaries. Doing this work and using these Tools helps you address hurts and move forward, which impacts, in beneficial ways, your physical and mental health. Work on forgiveness is essential for those who long for peace in the world and have the courage to begin with themselves.

The more you understand, the easier it is to forgive. The Strategies provided give you insights and provide the foundation to help you forgive whether you are feeling that you can't forgive or you're the one seeking forgiveness. As part of these Strategies, we include current research integrating psychological, sociological, spiritual, and developmental principles. We include cultural, religious, institutional, and legal issues that impact forgiving.

We also provide stories to help you see what this looks like in real life. With their permission, we use stories people have shared with us in our workshops or as part of our work. In the section "Then Comes Understanding," we link stories with the Tools and Strategies in a way that helps you understand and do your work.

When you're able to learn from your own story, you give yourself the freedom to look at what happened and work towards forgiving, especially in painful relationships. You're able to ask questions such as "Were there signs that I missed? Was my understanding of the relationship wrong? Were there problems in the relationship that I missed?"

When you have a sense of wholeness, you're able to integrate your rational mind with your feelings. Wholeness is neither coldly intellectual nor too emotional. You can then move on to more positive questions, such as "What can I learn from this? What are the teachings learned from this situation, or that relationship?"

We invite you to risk, to be open to new possibilities for living. Being open also means being surprised at the process and the conclusions. It is important to be open to using all the information and the Tools and Strategies offered here. We want you to be open to a new way of thinking, open to a different perspective so you can move forward in a way that is comfortable for you.

1

The Freedom Forgiving Brings

At some point, we all face issues of forgiving. At times, you may not know where to begin, especially with the tough issues. You can't begin if you're blocked by fear and frustration, or if you're wrestling with questions like these:

- Do I have to forgive?
- Do I even want to forgive?
- If I forgive, who benefits?
- Are some things simply unforgivable?
- Am I weak if I forgive?
- Will I disappoint family and friends, especially if it looks like the other person got away with something?
- Will it seem like a betrayal if I forgive?
- What happens when the person I want to forgive is no longer living?

Sometimes all you want is to get past what happened, but you remain caught in painful memories. You can't begin because your feelings refuse to fade. If you even think about forgiving, your anger surges all over again. This kind of frustration leaves you feeling powerless. Ironically, you begin to wonder if maybe something is wrong with you. At this point, you may ask, "Why bother?" The mistaken belief is that there is nothing you can do but continue to suffer.

Who Benefits by Forgiving?

Here's what you need to know: the person who forgives is the one who benefits. The person who forgives is the one who becomes free. Many people find this surprising or confusing. There is good reason for this: when you are forgiven, it feels like you're the one who benefits. The experience of feeling better when you're forgiven has deep roots in childhood. Later on, as an adult, you continue to feel better when you are forgiven. You may simply feel relief; the conflict is over.

This one-sided experience of forgiveness is why so many people don't understand that the person who benefits is the person who forgives. Their earliest understanding as children is that of being forgiven. Learning to forgive as the necessary other side of forgiveness comes later. Sadly, many do not learn this, and their experience as a forgiving person is limited.

It is not surprising that a limited, one-sided understanding of forgiveness locks you into not forgiving. If you think the other person will get away with something, you do not want them to benefit by forgiving them. Perhaps you think they don't deserve to be forgiven. By not understanding forgiveness and who benefits, you will be critical of other people who forgive. You will be especially critical, even angry, if you think what happened was unforgivable. If you do not understand that the person who forgives is the one who benefits, then forgiving does not makes sense. This is why others sometimes become as angry at the person who forgives as at the one who caused harm.

Forgiving Sets You Free

When you forgive, you free yourself mentally, physically, and spiritually. Forgiveness involves letting go of what you choose to let go of so that you're no longer bound by anger, bitterness, or fear, or locked in the grip of pain. When you let go and are open to new information, other options become possible. By forgiving, you allow for new freedom and possibilities in your relationships. As you let go of erroneous expectations about someone else, you're free to discover who the other person really is. By forgiving, you are in a sense able to see the person as they are, with their strengths and weaknesses, not as you want them to be.

These kinds of letting go – of your hurt feelings and your expectations of the other person – give you the freedom to relate to them in more authentic ways, or not at all. When you let go of your anger, you're able to more clearly see the person and relationship as it was. This clarity helps you determine whether you want to reconcile with the person who hurt you, or not. You are free to change the relationship ground rules, no longer bound by mistaken expectations or buried feelings.

Part of forgiving, whether you're the one who let go or you feel like you lost a relationship, is a grieving process. At some level, you have to come to terms with the fact that the relationship has changed: you may grieve your hopes and dreams for a marriage or long-term friendship, for example. When you see this kind of grief for the relationship as it once was as part of forgiving, you can move forward in healthy ways. Having this perspective helps you set boundaries where needed: for example, in unsafe or unhealthy situations.

Forgiveness sometimes involves letting go of mistaken beliefs, such as that forgiving is the same for everyone, regardless of the circumstances, or that forgiveness is a one-time event where you forgive and it is over. As we will see, the danger is that rather than feeling freed when you forgive, you become frustrated by recurring painful memories. If these continue to dominate your thoughts, you may experience anger months or even years later. This interferes with your ability to enjoy life. Your frustration that you thought it was over and done with stems from not knowing that it is a process where you deal with the pain and hurt as much as you are able to at a particular time.

Forgiving is an integral part of your inner healing process. This healing brings you greater freedom as you strengthen your ability to integrate difficult experiences without bitterness. When you are healed, you are free to reconnect with others without the weight of past baggage. Past issues do not bind you; a painful experience no longer drives your life or saps your energy. When you are able to forgive, you will not feel dominated by one event or defined by one tragedy in your life.

This will feel like moving from anger to a sense of peace, from being a victim to being a survivor, and ultimately will allow you to thrive. By forgiving, you are free to move forward.

Understanding the Complexities of Forgiveness

Like all complex human behaviours, forgiveness can't be easily summed up in a simple definition. To help people understand what forgiveness is, we use three different concepts:

- forgiveness as a *process*, with evidence-based information and research
- forgiveness as a *paradox*, with knowledge and wisdom gained over centuries and in diverse cultures, and
- forgiveness as *mystery*, based in spirituality.

Each of these concepts provides insights and new ways of thinking about forgiveness: not only to define it, but to help you understand it and bring it to life.

What Is Forgiveness?

Forgiveness is a complex process. It takes place on all levels – body, mind, and spirit – which directly impacts physical, mental, and spiritual well-being. By its very nature, forgiveness involves individual personality, emotions, perceptions, beliefs, and spirituality. It can also include working through underlying societal, cultural, or religious beliefs about forgiveness.

Each process of forgiveness is unique: people have their own forgiveness temperament based, in part, on how they respond to conflict and how they relate to others as a result of their experience, upbringing, and personality. Part of the process involves getting in touch with feelings and being able to express them appropriately. Forgiveness also requires being able to deal with different kinds of loss, including the loss of relationships and ideals. As with all loss, there is a related grieving process that is usually an unacknowledged part of forgiving. All of this takes time and energy.

The inner process of forgiveness becomes an outer one when it is externalized in word and deed, in interactions with other people. As such, the process impacts all relationships – personal, family, social, and professional. For many, forgiveness also affects spiritual relationships. Forgiveness is essential in their relationship with the Sacred Other, or God, as they seek to forgive others and to be forgiven.

These days, forgiveness increasingly plays a key role in relationships between groups of people. This process takes place, for example, when a government offers a formal apology to a group of people following some kind of mistreatment. As we will see later, forgiveness is related to but not the same as reconciliation. It is incorrect to use the terms "forgiveness" and "reconciliation" interchangeably, as they are two separate processes.

Forgiveness is more than a psychological, spiritual, or relational process; forgiveness is a paradox – two things that seem contradictory are both true. This helps us see things not in terms of either/or, but as both/and. For example, forgiving is both personal and relational. Forgiving happens not just within those involved, but also in an outer way, in the relationship. Forgiving is so easy that children can do it as part of everyday life, yet forgiving is so hard that adults struggle with it even on their deathbeds.

Forgiving is visible and not visible: it is seen in the words, actions, and interactions of those involved. Yet forgiving remains unseen, as it takes place on an inner level, hidden within the person who forgives. On one hand, forgiveness is a practical necessity of living with others; on the other, it is a profoundly spiritual experience.

Finally, forgiveness cannot be narrowly defined as a process, nor summed up by the paradoxes it contains. Forgiveness also embodies what is best described as mystery. Part of the mystery of forgiveness is its connection with humankind's highest ideals of peace, justice, and mercy. For the individual, the mystery of forgiving is linked with their integrity: the way they choose to live and their personal legacy.

Many spiritual traditions call forth the mystery of forgiveness as part of their teachings and sacred traditions. Most of the world's great religions call followers to forgive, yet forgiving is an individual process. Part of the mystery of forgiveness is that the act of forgiving brings forth peace and harmony. Forgiving multiplies as this peace inspires others, so its benefits extend far beyond those directly involved. For some, it remains a mystery that the person who forgives is the one who benefits. They cannot imagine that those who forgive experience a sense of peace or liberation, while those who don't forgive are bound by pain or anger.

To help you see the complexity of some of the forgiveness issues in the chapters ahead, we share Helen's story. It helps us understand real-life struggles. All the names of the people in the stories have been changed. Where necessary, circumstances have been altered to protect privacy.

Helen's Story: "I Can Forgive my Ex, but I Can't Forgive Her"

I share my story of how three people, my former husband and my two closest friends, shaped my life and my person. I don't claim to be innocent, but I felt like the loser in what became a triangle of relationships. In the end, I was the one not chosen.

The year my husband walked away was the worst and best year of my life. With the help of a therapist, I moved forward. But I couldn't begin to forgive my husband until I understood my part in it all.

I thrive when I honestly share my inner journey and in conversations working through the mysteries of life. However, when I first married, I felt this was unattainable. My husband, though a reflective person, never shared his inner journey, and I never expressed my need. This led me outside the marriage to seek meaning. It was okay when my closest relationships were with women.

From the beginning, I felt a connection with my friend Chuck that I'd never experienced with another person before. Much of the time Chuck and I spent together was with my family, so I thought there could be no harm. When I asked my husband, he denied that my being with Chuck made him unhappy or insecure. I was young and unaware of the communication problems developing in my marriage, and my husband didn't express any concerns.

My husband and I shared similar values; we were brought up going to church and we maintained our involvement. Over the years, I went through periods of questioning my capacity for a lifetime commitment to be happy and in love with the man I married. I reluctantly let go of my relationship with Chuck, the man who brought happiness to my life.

When I met Hazel, we quickly developed a wonderful friendship. We searched for meaning within our faith, and shared our struggles. Hazel, too, became a part of our family, sharing dinners and holidays.

I shared with Hazel my desire to be in love with my husband and my confusion about how easy it was to share my struggles with Chuck. It felt as if God put Hazel in my life for a reason. My connection with her allowed me to distance myself from Chuck.

Life got so busy that working on our marriage never became a priority. I focused on my children's lives, which allowed me to deny any problems in the marriage. My husband became disillusioned, but he was unwilling to share his inner journey with me. I thought he shut down his feelings towards me to spare himself the pain if I left the marriage. I began counselling and invited my husband to participate. In counselling, we never discussed my relationship with Chuck. My husband shared with me after the marriage ended that the pace we lived was an issue.

Although my husband once loved me more than I could accept, he fell in love with someone else. The last years of our marriage were a living hell for our entire family! The fact the other woman was Hazel, my closest friend, made the marriage breakdown even more difficult. I felt completely betrayed by the two people I had trusted most in my life. I wanted to die; the only thing that kept me pushing forward was the thought that my children needed me.

It was a low point; my only experience of depression had been seeing others live with it. For years, my husband had suffered from clinical depression. Never had I experienced that deep, dark place within until I slowed down enough to realize that what was happening outside was tearing me apart inside. In part, I feel depression visited me because I needed empathy to understand what my husband had been through. This could only help me to forgive him.

My journey to forgive him came after I understood my part and my pain in it all. I tried to involve him, but neither of us was at the point where that could happen. I required more time for healing. I needed distance from him and the situation. Anger followed the hurt. Each time I tried to meet with him, the wounds were reopened. Journalling helped me to express some of the intensity of feeling.

In the end, I made a decision to leave the area where I had grown up and lived out my marriage. A new city would allow a fresh start. Before I moved, I felt the need to write my husband a letter. As the words fell to the page, my forgiving was moving to a new place. I wasn't sure if I would ever send the letter, but I wanted him to hear the story from my perspective. I wanted him to know that I was sorry for the pain I had caused, and I wanted to help ease his guilt. I sent the letter with no expectations, with no hope or desire to receive a reply, and no reply came. In dropping the letter in the mailbox, I felt there was more progress towards the healing place, and in that moment, it felt as if forgiveness had taken place.

I moved away, giving my children the choice to come with me. One of my children found the decision very difficult. He didn't want to live away from me, but he didn't want to leave his life and his friends, either. Three months later, I was called back home, as he had attempted to take his life. This created the occasion to meet with his dad, and he brought up the letter. He apologized for not responding. He expressed his gratitude to me for having written and sent it. He asked if we could meet, and so we decided to come together and finally speak our realities in the context where the pain, hurt, and anger no longer lived in either of us. It was truly the end of a long road in forgiving each other.

To this day, I still feel sadness. It is more about the loss of a marriage than the loss of my husband. I believe that Hazel was not the cause of the breakdown, but a symptom of our unhealthy relationship. I have grown immensely through the process of healing. I sometimes wonder where I would be had our marriage not ended. The ending turned out to be a gift.

I am not sure it is possible to forgive Hazel. It's the last piece to truly move forward with my life. When I must meet my children's father and Hazel, who is now his new wife, I wish to meet without stress, worry, or wasted energy. My dilemma is that I have no desire to do this with the other woman. I long to forgive her for what she did, but I want to do so without involving her in a physical sense.

In sharing stories with others and through reflection, I realize that I connected forgiveness with reconciliation. I now try to imagine that forgiveness can take place independent of reconciliation. I tend to believe in my heart that in order to forgive another, that person must recognize that they have wronged you, and must be sorry and seek forgiveness. The process I went through to forgive my ex-husband took several years. For the most part, I did it independently of him. It had a timing of its own. No matter how I wanted it to go, it could not be rushed. It did not feel truly finished until we met and shared our perspectives free from the hurt and anger. It was a long meeting where we talked only briefly about the past, but it was clear that forgiveness was granted both ways. Comfort came with the forgiveness, knowing that meeting him in the future could happen without stress. I know I am a better person for having loved this man enough to work through the hurt and healing.

Eight years after our breakup, I found myself face to face with his wife for the first time since their marriage. In my new beginning,

I felt there was no need to heal that part of my life. She took no energy from me and consumed no thought, so I concluded it must be in the past.

Our eldest was getting married, and I began to stress about encountering the new wife. I could not imagine speaking to her, but there was a curious sense of wanting to see the two of them together for the first time as a married couple. I stressed about seeing her in the smaller context of the events leading up to the wedding. The rehearsal dinner was going to be my first encounter.

As they arrived at the event, I retreated upstairs and watched them come up to the house together. I wanted them to come in and get comfortable. As I took some extra time, I settled and got myself together to join the festivities. I decided the easiest way was to go and say hello to my former husband's parents. As I turned to walk away after greeting my in-laws, Hazel, my former closest friend, jumped into my path and held out her arms in a gesture to embrace. She was offering a hug!

All that passed through me in that brief moment cannot be articulated. It was panic and a cold sickness in my centre. I knew that everyone's eyes were on us, and I thought quickly about how I could pass through this politely and remain true to my inner feelings. I could not let her hug me, and I could not look into her eyes. The betrayal I felt was as intense as it had been the day I saw my former husband's car in her driveway a few short weeks after he had left me. It all flooded back into me in that moment. I could not let her hug me. I extended my hand quickly and grabbed hers and politely said, "It is nice to see you, too, and it has been a long time." I turned away quickly, feeling sick but not wanting to dampen the spirit of celebration. The reason for the gathering had to come first. I reminded myself that this was not about my relationship with her.

She kept a healthy distance after our brief encounter. Looking back, I felt sad about the loss of what we had, and sad that I probably hurt her in that exchange. I found it difficult to understand how she could expect me to hug her. I assumed this means she believes she did nothing wrong. How can forgiveness begin when she doesn't believe it is necessary? Or was she thinking forgiveness could take place in that embrace?

The weeks following the wedding brought me many a thought about forgiveness. How can I begin to forgive her? I don't want future meetings to be an issue: she will always be there, and I will forever wonder what the next encounter will be like. I wish to control those meetings. I question if I am ready to forgive her. I know it cannot be rushed. I can't tell myself how to feel, even though I try.

The ability to forgive my former husband comes with the fact that I played a part in the hurt. Maybe my inability to forgive his new wife comes from my belief that I did nothing to her except make clear her place in the mess of my marriage. I am surprised that the betrayal still feels so potent after so many years.

We will return to Helen's story in the following chapters to help you understand the complexity of forgiveness. Many people share Helen's struggle with the anguish of divorce and with feelings of betrayal, anger, and guilt.

2

Forgiving: Knowing Where and How to Begin

L ife can be messy, with more than enough opportunities for misunderstanding, betrayal, and conflict. We need to learn how to get along in today's increasingly complex and multicultural world. It's sad that we don't really understand forgiving, considering the disagreement that happens in families, within marriages, between friends, within communities, and so on. Learning about forgiveness is one of the most important things you can do for your well-being and for your relationships.

Tools and Strategies for Healing, Moving Forward, and Forgiveness

Forgiving touches each of us differently. As we saw in Chapter 1, forgiving is a deeply personal process. Beginning to deal seriously with forgiveness is hard work; it involves your personality, your self-concept, your sense of self-worth, as well as ideas related to your cultural or religious upbringing. The freedom of forgiveness comes as you address areas that block you. As you begin to understand, and remove these obstacles by using the Tools and Strategies (T/S), you bring healing in your own time and in your own way.

Throughout the book, we emphasize that forgiveness is a process, rather than a one-time event. Each stage of the process requires you to embrace different tasks. Having the right Tools for these tasks brings you a sense of empowerment. As you make use of the Tools and Strategies, you will experience increased competency, giving you the energy to work through previous blocks.

Even though the Tools and Strategies are numbered for your convenience, forgiveness is not a linear process. You may find some of them easier than others. It is likely you'll use them differently as you gain more experience. For example, you may become aware of how tense your body becomes when writing, or sharing your story about what happened. Rather than ignore this tension, as you probably did in the past, you now decide to exercise, practise yoga, or work with a massage therapist to alleviate painful physical tension.

We recommend you keep a "forgiveness journal" that is strictly for your own use. Use it to note your feelings and your struggle, or as a way to keep track of the work you do with the Tools and Strategies. At first, you may find yourself questioning what you are doing. This may be due to what psychologists call "resistance." This is a normal part of the process. You have made the first step: simply starting the process of forgiveness helps bring about a healing environment.

T/S 1: PREPARE THE GROUNDWORK TO FORGIVE

Once you've made the decision to begin, the first step is to ground your forgiveness work in respect. Respect is an integral part of the process and requires more than lip service. Make every effort to be respectful in your thoughts and what you do. This begins with respecting yourself. Build respect for each person involved, for the situation, for communications, for your vulnerability, and for the process.

Respect Yourself

You may be thinking, this is easy; I already respect myself. Respect for yourself includes acknowledging when you are hurt. No one should minimize this. Having respect for yourself means that you don't say things like "It doesn't really matter" or "It's no big deal" when the truth is that it did matter, and as a result you were upset or hurt. Having respect means you don't deny your feelings. But this does not suggest that you have to blurt out your feelings. When you respect yourself, you have even more control over your actions because you do not deny or repress your feelings.

When you respect yourself, you have more self-knowledge because you look closely at your feelings to see what makes you tick. As part of this respect-for-self, you need to look at how you tend to be hurt by others. It is hard for couples, for example, where one person tends to be sensitive and the other person is not. The person who is accused of being overly sensitive may be aware of, and may acknowledge, his or her hurt. Generally, when you're told you're being oversensitive, the subtle message is that you are doing something wrong. If so, over time, this has a tendency to shut you down so it becomes difficult to respect your feelings. This also happens if you are criticized for being oversensitive because you are passionate about something; you believe in what you are doing. It could be that the other person has no feelings about something you care deeply about. The danger in being oversensitive is that your feelings overpower your thinking and you undermine your ability to work through relationship issues.

Problems also arise in relationships if you are dismissed because you are seen as overreacting. The difference in being oversensitive and overreactive is this: being oversensitive is an emotional response; being overreactive means you act out. When you act out, you are not in control. Having respect for yourself means looking at your thoughts and responses without dismissing or denying them because you value yourself. This kind of self-respect is based in self-knowledge, and as a result you are in control.

Respect the Other Person

Respect for the other person begins by affirming his or her dignity as a human being. Relationships, by their very nature, open you to the possibility of being hurt. The closer you are to someone, the more power they have to hurt you – accidentally or on purpose. When you base forgiving in respect, you become more aware that there may be reasons for the other person's actions. At the simplest level, respect for the other helps you see what you have in common; after all, we all make mistakes, and you, too, have no doubt hurt others at times.

In terms of the forgiveness process, respect for the person who hurt you does not mean you have to like that person. To respect the person who hurt you can be difficult. But if you don't try, you run the risk of demonizing them. Without respect for the other person, you also miss opportunities to forgive. Having respect for the other person does not mean you have to reconcile with them. Nor does this make you responsible for their behaviour. This respect for the other is based on truth; here, too, you do not deny what happened, or make excuses for the other person.

Respect Your Experience

When you respect your experience, you do not trivialize or deny what happened. Rather, you choose to look honestly at what happened – in terms of your emotions and the impact on your life now and in the future. This involves finding out what your experience means by looking at questions such as "Why is this getting to me?" There may be a link between a seemingly trivial issue and a significant one in your life. By paying attention to your thoughts and feelings, you will find the deeper issue. When you respect your experience, you won't take responsibility for a situation over which you have no control. You have more options to handle your feelings about the situation and how you choose to deal with it.

Respect the Power of Words

All of your good intentions are meaningless if your words add to the conflict. This is why, for example, some couples take time to learn how to "fight fair" when they argue. When respect begins with what you say and how you speak, respect for your actions more easily follows. Because developing respect for the power of words is hard to put into practice, we have included a whole section, *Non-labelling Language and Sacred Listening*, to provide you with powerful tools and communication skills. These will help you communicate so your intentions align with your words.

Respect Your Security and Vulnerability Issues

As you work on forgiving, you must take care to respect your areas of vulnerability. This requires becoming aware of what these are. This is not always easy; it takes courage to find your sore spots. Forgiving becomes more difficult if you have a history of being hurt. It's understandable to feel "Once bitten, twice shy" or say, "I'm not going there again." In both cases, you'll be less likely to take risks with new relationships, and you'll have a tendency to self-protect in all your relationships. Keep in mind that if your vulnerability issues are related to your security, it is best to seek outside help.

Respect Your Forgiving Process

Respect for the process means taking the time and using the energy required for forgiveness. Forgiveness is complicated; variables may include the amount of damage done; the particular kind of relationship; pain suffered; and related grief and guilt. These impact the time you need for healing and forgiving. When you respect the process, you acknowledge that you may be blocked for some reason. While you acknowledge that wanting to forgive is not enough, you don't rush it. And you don't berate yourself if you can't immediately forgive. Respecting the process allows you to become more in touch with changes in how you feel, and with the relationship itself.

T/S 2: WRITE YOUR STORY: TELL WHAT HAPPENED

The first step in forgiving is telling what happened. This is critical. Write your story in your own words and in your own way. As this is strictly for your own use, don't be concerned with spelling or technique. ➤

Writing what happened is a way to honour your story and to respect yourself. Pay attention to what comes first in your memory. Try not to censor yourself or control your writing. If this is the first time you have done this, especially if you've kept secret what happened, find a place for privacy. Even if you've told others what happened, set aside time to write without being interrupted or rushed.

Take note of your thoughts and feelings as you write. Writing helps organize your thoughts and allows emotions to come to the surface in a safe way. Although accessing your emotions in this way makes the process easier, it can still be difficult. You may feel overwhelmed by your emotional response. If you need a break, take the time you need and return to writing your story when your feelings have subsided. Once you've finished, set your story aside for later reflection.

After using all the Tools and Strategies, return to your story and look at the issues related to forgiveness. This makes it easier to handle any roadblocks.

Why Is It So Hard to Forgive?

Why is forgiving so difficult? Why are there roadblocks? Keep in mind that forgiveness is complex, and betrayal is one of the more hurtful human experiences. It's easier to say why you "don't want to" forgive than figure out why you "can't" forgive. You may be blocked by fear or depression. Perhaps you harbour anger or have become bitter, which confuses your efforts. What appears to be an inability to forgive can sometimes be a form of grieving. You may have to grieve lost expectations and your hopes and dreams for a relationship that is important to you. When you don't understand this kind of loss, this impedes your forgiving process.

When you want to forgive, but you can't, this can feel like you're weak. When you don't deal with issues, you may say things like, "Don't go there! Leave it alone." The longer you struggle, the greater the sense of failure. The resultant stress shows up in your body as tension or anxiety. As a result, especially when combined with repressed anger, you run greater risk of developing stress-related illnesses. Research shows that stress contributes to diseases such as diabetes, addictions, eating disorders, and heart disease.

T/S 3: TAKE STOCK: WHAT DO YOU BRING TO THE FORGIVENESS TABLE?

You will clarify your initial thinking about forgiveness as you use this self-evaluation. As a general rule, the best approach to using the Tools and Strategies is to decide to do this with an open mind, letting your ideas flow. Be as honest as you can. These questions help you to get in touch with where you are now, which helps you decide where you want to go. You may want to save your answers in your journal for later use.

- Did you see forgiving as a sign of weakness? If so, why?
- Were you afraid that forgiving meant forgetting what happened?
- Did you worry you would betray others if you were to forgive?
- Were there times where you felt you were forced to forgive? Did it work for you or the other person?
- Is forgiving an embarrassing thing to do? Is it too emotional? Can you explain why?
- If you were not able to forgive in the past, what do you think prevented you? Be specific.
- Were there any situations where you wanted something else to happen before you could forgive?
- Were you afraid forgiving meant nothing would improve or change in your life?
- Were you afraid forgiving meant nothing would change in a relationship?
- Are you ready to forgive?

Your answers help put you in touch with your emotions, expectations, values, and beliefs. Even if you are surprised by what you have written, these responses give you helpful insights. You now have new information about yourself and, hopefully, can make way for new options in your life. Based on your answers, and now that you know where you are, it's healthy to acknowledge that you may not want to forgive. However, once you've made the choice to forgive, it's a different matter; you give yourself more options. You may have unfinished business and unresolved issues that must be addressed. Perhaps you sense something is not what it appears to be.

Your pain is yours; nobody has the right to dismiss it. Forgiving doesn't imply that you forget or minimize what you went through. No one has the right to judge you or give you unsolicited advice. Even with professional help, ultimately only you can address your pain to bring about resolution and healing. As indicated in T/S 1, when you respect yourself, the situation, and the process, you acknowledge your struggle as a necessary part of life rather than seeing it as a failure.

Forgive or Not: What Do Other People Think?

You will feel more at peace when forgiving is not externally driven or demanded. When you feel forced, or the motivation isn't really yours, the risk is that internal conflict arises. This is where guilt about not forgiving and self-blame often stem from. You may be told, for example, "You *have to* forgive for the sake of the family" or "You're heart attack material! You *have to* forgive, forget about it, and move on."

As mentioned, when you don't want to forgive, you may have good reasons. We will explore these in depth in later chapters. You face other kinds of problems if you think you should forgive, but can't, no matter how much you would like to. As we will see, forgiveness cannot simply be commanded, demanded, or faked. However, by making a conscious decision to forgive, you have taken an important first step towards freedom. You have begun your own process of healing.

Things You Can Change and Things You Can't

When you're able to move beyond just being resigned to a place of acceptance, you've taken the first step to move on with your life. This is part of the wisdom in the Serenity Prayer: "God grant me the serenity to accept the things I cannot change; the courage to change the things I can; and the wisdom to know the difference." This is why, as you begin forgiveness work, you acknowledge in what ways you were hurt and how deeply you were hurt.

We stress that acceptance doesn't mean that whatever happened is okay, or that you won't do anything about it. The point is this: once you have accepted that it has happened, you can begin to do something about it with realistic expectations about how to address issues, often with a growing sense of calm. Acceptance helps move you beyond being resigned to your fate so you suffer fewer flare-ups, and feel hurt and angry less often. With acceptance, you're able to focus on what you have achieved and the lessons you've learned as part of the process.

What's Your Part in the Situation?

Some people blame others rather than deal with the issue. They feel better because they don't have to take responsibility for their actions. It is always someone else's fault, or the fault of the system, but this comes at a cost, as it stops meaningful attempts to address the problem. Sadly, for those whose blaming others becomes deeply ingrained, they hurt themselves and damage their relationships: any kind of meaningful forgiveness or reconciliation becomes impossible as issues are not addressed.

Scapegoating is not an isolated or individual problem. French philosopher René Girard says this tendency to blame others is deeply embedded within humankind. All too often, one group blames another group for its problems, or as being the cause of a natural disaster: for example, the killing of Christians in the Roman Empire, the burning of witches during the Middle Ages in Europe, and modern-day blaming natural disasters on people with HIV/AIDS. Sadly, even when evidence shows otherwise, the real causes are not addressed, and solutions to the problem are not found. Eventually, this leads to situations where one group realizes it has hurt another group and tries to repair the damage, most often by making an official public apology. (We will address this situation later.)

Self-blame versus Taking Responsibility

Taking responsibility for your actions is healthy; blaming yourself tends to be destructive. In terms of forgiveness, when you take responsibility for your actions, you can begin to address problems. With self-blame, you have already decided that you are the problem and the solution in one closed circle. You may simply end up feeling worse. For example, in situations where you can't forgive, you blame yourself because you feel like a phony going through the motions: "There's something wrong with me." No matter what, you blame yourself, which makes you feel worse, not better; this only makes it harder to address forgiveness issues constructively. When you take responsibility, you are more open to advice on how to deal with the issue, even if you are feeling stuck.

Shouldn't the Other Person Ask for Your Forgiveness?

There is another hidden way to blame others; you set this up by making your actions dependent on what the other person does. It is easy to blame the person you can't forgive because they didn't do something you wanted. This kind of blaming effectively thwarts forgiving, as your entire focus is on the other person. You're not free as long as you expect someone else to take the initiative; you will feel blocked or angry. The other person might never do what you want; they might think it is you who should do something. If you think the other person should have known better or feel that they have to say sorry before you forgive, you've given up your ability to forgive and based it on their behaviour. Worse yet, you give up control over your peace of mind and, to some degree, control of your own well-being. The danger is that you become an "if" person, where you forgive if the person does what you expect them to do. Once you understand that forgiving is your choice, not theirs, you're in control.

What If You're Wrong When You Blame Others?

You make a lot of assumptions by thinking the other person is entirely to blame for what happened. What if your assumptions are wrong? What if you assumed the other person had all the necessary information when the hurtful event occurred? What if you assumed, falsely, that the other person knew beforehand the consequences of their actions? What if they have a different point of view about what happened, or believe they have valid reasons for their behaviour? Sometimes, no matter how much you regret that what you assumed to be true turns out to be wrong, too much water has gone under the bridge. The result is that you have irreparably damaged a relationship and created a whole other level of forgiving issues.

We are all limited in our point of view. It is better to give others the benefit of the doubt until you have all the facts. By trying to keep an open mind, you're able to see other perspectives, and when you do, you gain power and have more control. By having more control over your actions, you also have more control over the situation. With more information, you have more options to respond appropriately to the other person and to the situation.

Removing Obstacles to Forgiving

The masks or personas we assume in different social circumstances serve a useful purpose. We all change our behaviour depending on the circumstances; we dress to meet certain expectations. We expect professionals to dress differently at work; we expect them to speak and act accordingly. Sometimes we joke that we accidentally used our inside voice, which shows what we're really thinking, when we meant to use our outside voice in that situation.

Problems arise when these masks get in the way, hiding our true self. It can also create problems when we don't realize that these masks cause us to project onto people in our lives what we need or want them to be. Over time, these projections can get in the way in relationships. Sometimes we remove our projections. Long-time married couples sometimes talk about falling in love all over again, as one or both of them come to love their partner as they really are, warts and all. This happens, for example, when a spouse withdraws their projections to discover another side of their spouse that is even more attractive. It's also possible for the opposite to happen: a spouse realizes they are in love with a projection of their own making. Withdrawing projections in relationships can be painful or it can be freeing as you see more clearly, without interference.

T/S 4: DETERMINE YOUR GOALS: WHAT DO YOU WANT TO ACHIEVE?

If you want to forgive, envisioning your goals takes you one step closer. Answering these questions helps clarify your goals:

1. How will you feel if you forgive? Will forgiving reduce your anguish, your pain? Will you be less upset about the situation?

2. Will forgiving help you let go? What does letting go mean to you?

3. If you forgive, will this reduce the suffering of others?

4. When you forgive, what do you expect of the person you forgave? What changes in behaviour do you need from them?

5. If you forgive, will your relationship change? What are your new expectations about the relationship?

6. Do you have any specific goals connected to forgiving? (For example, you will be able to be in the presence of your ex-spouse for the sake of your children.)

What Makes You Tick?

The more you understand what makes you tick, the more control you have over your actions. It's been said that "You can't change what you don't know." Whether you know it or not, part of forgiving is based in your assumptions and expectations. By looking at these, you have more options and more control of your actions, especially when you struggle with painful issues.

Core Values

Our values flow from the core of our being; that's why we refer to our "core values." Your assumptions are part of your core; your expectations are not. This is why it's harder to change your assumptions (your core values) than to change your expectations (which are not core). Here is another way of looking at this: your assumptions are near and dear to your heart, so they're hard to change. It's easier to change distant expectations, because they flow from your core assumptions and so are more removed. It is also easier to change expectations because they are more specific than assumptions.

No one wilfully and consciously chooses blindness or ignorance. Let's look at an example, an assumption based in gender: chauvinism is an *assumption* about superiority. Normally, superiority is related to one's own cause, group, or gender. A man who is a male chauvinist *assumes* men are superior to women. Based on this assumption, he has an *expectation* that men are more competent than women. This leads to difficulty dealing with women in positions of power or professional authority. By and large, when a male chauvinist encounters a professional or talented woman, he sees her as an *exception*, so he doesn't have to change his assumption about superiority.

When you look at your assumptions and expectations, you can overcome blocks, not only in forgiving, but in relationships. If a woman has a gender-based assumption that men are not to be trusted, this affects her relationships with men in general and with individual men. Each bad experience with men confirms her assumption. As a result, as she expects the worst in men, she acts accordingly in all her relationships. If, on the other hand, her assumption is that men are trustworthy, when she meets one who is not trustworthy, this affects just that particular relationship. In this case, her relationship with men as a whole is not affected by one bad experience.

Psychologists have studied why people don't change their assumptions in the face of contradictory information. They use the term "confirmation bias" to describe how people receive information that confirms their assumptions and exclude contradictory information. As an example, people with race-based assumptions have a different set of expectations for people of other races. Racists hold on to their assumptions (prejudices) regardless of what other information they receive. They can't see reality; they're controlled by their assumptions.

Generally, we feel threatened when one of our personal assumptions is threatened. This might lead to having to question other assumptions, which leads to the prospect of change. We seem to intuitively know that when we change our assumption, we change our behaviour. But we all resist change. This is why we defend our core assumptions; when our assumptions are threatened, we experience stress.

As with all threats, we want to minimize the threat in any way possible. We attack the messenger rather than listen to the message. We respond by saying things like "What does he know?" or "She's *just* a woman." We do anything to avoid stress or change, even though our denial often creates more stress.

Throughout history, many great spiritual teachers were perceived to be dangerous precisely because they challenged commonly held assumptions of that time and culture. Those in power were threatened when great leaders such as Gandhi, Jesus, Muhammad, or Buddha challenged assumptions about justice, equality, and fairness. They challenged assumptions about power and how we treat others. In most societies, the poor do not share the same assumptions and expectations as the rich and powerful. This is one of the reasons why those without power are better able to hear what spiritual leaders have to say.

Much of the progress in the world occurs when a spiritual or social leader challenges assumptions. In the 1960s, Martin Luther King challenged misguided assumptions about African Americans' leadership and role in society. As history shows, challenging commonly held assumptions can involve great personal risk.

How Your Perceptions Impact Forgiving

As we've seen, how you live and how you relate to others are rooted, in part, in your assumptions and expectations. Problems arise if, for example, your assumption is that forgiving means overlooking or forgetting a terrible event, as this prevents you from even thinking about forgiving – even though this is a false assumption. This is why it is often helpful to talk to someone about your experience, as you get the benefit of seeing through their eyes.

Sharing does not mean a gripe session where you complain and reinforce negative feelings. Those who *need* others to agree with their point of view aren't always looking for solutions, and they don't want to forgive. They become stuck because they avoid anything that threatens their perception of what happened.

The key point for forgiveness is that two people can have very different interpretations of what happened. It is as if each one sees through a different pair of glasses, which leaves lots of room for misunderstanding and hurt feelings. No two people see an event exactly the same way. This is why in marriage therapy, for example, part of the therapist's work is to help clients understand that each partner has their own perception of the same event.

We all focus on details important to us and ignore those aspects that don't fit. It's as if we wear a personalized lens that acts as a filter between us and the actual event. Our lens is made up of our assumptions, expectations, and emotions. We also see events filtered through our personal history, our goals, and our values. In a sense, we see what we want to see. Sometimes these lenses not only cloud our perception, they alter it. There are times when these filters are self-limiting, even dangerous. Sometimes, your expectations about another person become self-fulfilling prophecies. Say, for example, that you have an acquaintance, Wayne, whom you think is cold and unfriendly. As a result, you're guarded and withdrawn when you meet him. In turn, your behaviour causes Wayne to feel uncomfortable; as a result, he's cold and distant. Your perception of Wayne as unfriendly becomes a self-fulfilling prophecy.

In addition to personal filters, there are also group filters. Cultural, societal, and religious beliefs also act as filters that impact forgiving. These kinds of filtering beliefs occur between individuals and whole groups or classes of people. For example, if it's a commonly held belief that politicians are greedy and dishonest, your opinion is preformed even when you meet a politician who is dedicated to public service. These kinds of filters label groups of people based on differences in culture, race, or gender, regardless of the individual person or in spite of contrary facts. Sadly, far too often throughout history, one race or cultural group suffers at the hands of another group because of mistaken or dangerous assumptions.

Rachel's Story: "I Could Forgive, So Why Can't I Forget?"

We chose Rachel's story to show how the filters, her assumptions and expectations, affected her life. Rachel sought answers because none of her friendships lasted, no matter how hard she tried. Rachel shared how sad it made her feel that she was always the one who put more energy into relationships. The breaking point for her was yet another painful experience. She explains:

Tanya and I had been friends for a long time, and good friends for over five years. We spent a lot of time together, and not just at work. It meant a lot to share our thoughts and feelings. Even after I changed jobs, and even though we both had crazy busy lives and less time, when we got together, it was like no time had passed.

We always remembered each other's birthdays. I have to admit I made special efforts on hers. When we couldn't get together, I made a point to phone and wish her Happy Birthday.

The first time she forgot my birthday I was surprised and a little hurt. But I thought, hey, that happens. The next year, she forgot again – completely forgot: no late card, no call, nothing. I wasn't just hurt, I was angry. It bothered me. Why did she forget mine when I always remembered hers? Why was this a big deal for me, but not for her? I was tired of doing all the work.

Later, we ran into each other, and she asked to catch up. I don't know why, but I told her what bothered me. Tanya seemed surprised. She said she hardly had time to remember her own birthday. I told her it was no big deal, but deep down, it hurt. The thing was, why do things like this bother me so much? Why was it me who was always the one who ended up feeling stupid or feeling hurt?

Are You Actually in Charge?

Rachel didn't realize how much she expected her friends to act in ways she thought they should. Rachel's assumption was that close friends remembered birthdays. Rachel also expected Tanya to do something to make up for forgetting; Tanya's saying she was sorry wasn't enough. Rachel told herself she forgave Tanya, but she was still angry and she couldn't forget. This bothered her, as she thought of herself as a forgiving person.

Then Comes Understanding

When Rachel was able to see that it was her own assumption, not Tanya's, that close friends should remember birthdays, she also saw that she expected Tanya to do what she herself wanted, and her unmet expectation made her angry. At a deeper level, Rachel realized she thought forgetting meant that Tanya didn't value their friendship; Rachel's lingering anger and struggle to forgive was connected to feeling unappreciated and undervalued.

This was not the first time Rachel experienced this feeling of being let down by a friend. This was like a lightning rod for her anger, because she felt she was the one who did all the work in relationships. Until Rachel was able to see the disconnect between her expectations and her assumptions about what her friend should do, she couldn't see that her reactions were out of proportion to what had happened. In the past, Rachel couldn't figure out why she felt miserable and guilty at the same time, even though she didn't think it was her fault. Rachel felt relief when she understood more about herself and how she interacted with friends.

Rachel became aware of her own fears and the pain of not being valued. This helped her to address deeper issues, not just birthdays. Rachel didn't think she was needy or realize how quickly she blamed others for what happened. Eventually, not only was she able to forgive her friend, she had more clarity about her sense of vulnerability and self-worth. She felt she would no longer be triggered in the same way. This gave Rachel more confidence to let go and move on in other friendships.

What If Someone Won't Forgive You?

Sometimes you feel as if you do everything right, and still the other person won't forgive you. Remember, you can't demand to be forgiven; more than that, you must recognize their choice not to forgive. It might be that the other person is simply not ready to forgive at that time. However, there are times when not being forgiven indicates the need for further reflection on your part. Perhaps the other person doubts your sincerity in asking, especially if you have something to gain. Do you have a history that makes them doubt if you've changed? Whatever the situation, if the other person will not forgive you and you have done all that you can, give them time to work through the issue.

Culturally Based Assumptions about Forgiveness

Culture also affects forgiveness: some cultures are orientated towards the individual, while others have a collective orientation. For cultures with a communal perspective, forgiving becomes complicated, as any instance of forgiveness involves more than the individuals directly involved. In this case, when you offend one person, by extension, you offend the whole family: the offense is not limited to the offended person. These kinds of offenses become deadly serious when understood to be an offense against the entire family, tribe, or clan. In some cultures, the shared assumption is that there can be no forgiveness, only retribution or revenge. Someone needs to be punished in order to restore family honour or maintain the balance of power between groups.

In today's world, it's important to look at your own cultural perspective (your assumptions and expectations) about forgiveness so you're able to recognize differences. This is part of enacting the respect we talked about in T/S 1. You'll make things worse by acting as if the other person's perspective on forgiveness is less important than yours.

If you encounter differences, asking appropriate questions helps you clarify the issues. If you've offended someone, ask questions such as "Please help me understand. What does this incident mean to you? What can I do to rectify the situation?" While you can't expect to be familiar with everyone's cultural assumptions and expectations, it's important to try and find out what would help the other person.

Roadblocks to Forgiving: Irrational Beliefs and Unrealistic Expectations

We saw how our view of the world is filtered through our emotions, expectations, and assumptions. Now we look at the role of internalized beliefs, especially dysfunctional ones, in our lives. This is hard work, as most often your first reaction when one of your internalized beliefs is challenged is to become defensive. Looking within as objectively as possible, and handling this reaction, is part of the hard work in forgiving.

Deeply entrenched beliefs, however dysfunctional, are seldom questioned, yet they negatively impact your life. For example, you may have an internalized belief that wrong behaviour can't be forgiven without being punished. It might be that, as a child, you were *always* punished whenever you did something wrong, no matter how minor it was. You may have grown up believing that punishment is the only legitimate response to wrongdoing. This belief is entrenched, so it affects your expectations whether you're the one seeking forgiveness or doing the forgiving. It may also contribute to an unconscious desire to be punished before you can begin to feel forgiven. In other words, deep down, you equate punishment with being forgiven, even if you would not express it that way. This can frustrate you when your need to punish or be punished is not met.

Internalized beliefs can also be rooted in group or cultural beliefs. For example, in some cultures, the shared belief is that the person who hurt you must pay for or suffer for what they did. The fear is that the person looks stronger if you don't punish them, or the expectation that the wrongdoer will be able to hurt you again if you don't get revenge or punish them. Without knowing your personal or cultural internalized beliefs about forgiving, it becomes more difficult to forgive on your own terms.

Where Did that Come From?

The following 11 questions help you look at some of the commonly held beliefs and assumptions about forgiveness and identify roadblocks. If you like, use your journal to record your answers before reading the brief comments below the question. We address each of these questions in greater detail in later chapters.

1. Does forgiving means forgetting what happened?

Forgetting what happened isn't necessarily a good thing, let alone a healthy response. When you're not able to forget, this doesn't mean that something is wrong with you. On the contrary, it could be a helpful signal to make sure that justice is carried out. It could signal your desire to help protect others so that what happened to you won't happen to anyone else.

The fact that you remember signifies its importance. You don't want to forget because the experience has taught you something valuable: you know more about the person who hurt you and about life in general. It may point to the depth of your hurt. With this knowledge, you're able to move on; the hurtful event is just part of your life history. When you're able to move on without denial, you avoid becoming bitter.

Memories, however painful, have the potential to become a source of strength for you and others so you're able to share what you have experienced as a way to help others. Those who don't remember the past are doomed to repeat it. Your life experience – good and bad – becomes a source of wisdom.

2. Is it my duty to forgive?

Most children were told they have to forgive when someone says, "I'm sorry." To be good, they must forgive. They internalize this belief; later on, as adults, their expectation is that it's their duty to forgive.

You will see how beneficial it is for your entire well-being when you forgive, especially when forgiving stems from a genuine desire to forgive and you go through the necessary steps to address the issues. Going through the motions out of duty, or glossing over what happened, does no good; this approach disrespects your experience and the other person's. You cannot fully forgive if you do not engage all aspects of the process. You also can't have a real reconciliation when the underlying issues remain.

3. Does forgiving let the offender get away with it?

Remember, when you forgive, you're making a choice about *your* actions; not the offender's actions. There are times when what happened seems unforgivable. There are times when someone has done something so heinous that you are repulsed. Their actions seem cruel, perhaps even evil. Let's be clear: forgiving does not provide, in any way whatsoever, a free pass for their actions. Even if you forgive, this does not mean criminals should be exempt from the consequences of the law. Even if you choose to forgive, the person involved must be held accountable for their actions. Nor do you have to forget what happened. Forgiveness is about your healing and your choice, not someone else's. Remember, the one who benefits is the one who forgives, not the other way around.

4. If I forgive, am I condoning what happened?

There is a fear that if you forgive, you condone what happened, especially in serious matters. Forgiving points to the actions of the one who forgives; in no way does it deny wrongdoing. You are not responsible for the other person's actions. You are responsible only for your actions, which can include seeking justice for harm and holding others accountable for their actions.

5. If I forgive, will I prevent justice from being carried out?

When you are facing this fear, it is helpful to remember that forgiveness is an internal, individual process, not a legal one. There are well-known situations where, for example, a parent chooses to forgive their child's murderer, yet demands that the offender be brought to justice and face the consequences of their actions.

6. If I forgive, will I be victimized all over again?

The fear is that if you forgive, you will be revictimized. The truth is just the opposite. When you forgive out of choice, forgiving empowers you. You gain control of your own thoughts, your own actions, your own healing.

7. Is forgiveness a sign of weakness?

Fear can paralyze you, keeping you from doing what you want to do. Forgiveness requires making a choice. The best choices support your well-being and integrity. Those who label people who forgive as weak do not realize how much strength and courage is needed, or they think that if you forgive, nothing has changed. Remember, reconciliation is a separate process from forgiving. You don't have to reconcile, even when you have forgiven someone. You have options, including choosing to reconcile when, and how, it's appropriate and safe for you. Making a choice to forgive in the context of a possible reconciliation indicates strength, not weakness. Even with forgiving, you take into consideration factors such as "What do I need the person who hurt me to know about what happened (how they hurt me)? What changes do I want?"

8. Are women more forgiving than men?

As with many generalizations, this one doesn't hold up against the research. In one study, for example, preliminary research indicates that female judges give out more severe sentences than male judges in capital crimes. It's more useful, both in personal terms and in the workplace, to consider the characteristics of the individual man or woman rather than expecting them to conform to expectations solely based on gender.

Some of the men we have counselled felt blindsided when their wife wanted a divorce, even when the man wanted to salvage the marriage.

They found it hard to get over their bitterness that their wife chose to leave them. They were shocked, as this didn't match their assumptions or their expectations about women's behaviour.

9. If I try hard enough, can I forgive?

The mistaken assumption is that if you can't forgive, it's your problem. The implication is that there is something wrong with you. Your inability to forgive may reflect how badly you were hurt and your need to address deeper issues. There are times when the best decision is to get professional help. Carrying an unresolved issue is exhausting, diminishing your energy and sense of fulfillment.

10. Will my sincerity guarantee that I will be forgiven?

Many people believe that if they're sincere, the other person will forgive them. If you think it's your right to be forgiven, the unstated assumption is that not only should they forgive you – they have to forgive you. As we have seen, forgiving is based in choice, not duty. When you are asking for forgiveness, begin with T/S 1: respect that the person you hurt has their own time and pace needed to address the issues that perhaps you didn't see or expect.

Your demand to be forgiven because you are sincere is a form of revictimizing the other person. You are indicating that their thoughts, feelings, and actions count less than yours do. In fact, the way to show true sincerity is by your willingness to give them the time they need to forgive.

11. Will revenge restore my power?

Some people work on the assumption that seeking revenge (rather than seeking justice) shows strength. They have taken forgiveness off the table, as they fear they will look weak if they don't extract some form of punishment or retribution. Their expectation is that getting revenge restores personal power. This locks people into actions they may not want and takes away their choice about forgiving, which is a different kind of weakness.

3

The Difference between Forgiveness and Reconciliation

Most people feel comfortable talking about reconciliation, as we learn about this as children. It feels familiar: we know what reconciliation feels like when it happens. But we run into problems when we mistakenly think forgiveness and reconciliation are the same thing. Although they are related, they are separate processes with distinct characteristics.

We saw in Chapter 1 that forgiving is an inner process – it takes place within the person. Even though you can forgive entirely on your own, you cannot reconcile on your own. Reconciliation is an external process; it takes place between individuals. Just as forgiving is personal, each reconciliation is unique to the individuals who reconcile. Even though relationships share similar characteristics, each friendship, partnership, or marriage is one of a kind. There are times when reconciliation is not only a bad idea, it is dangerous. There are times when it is necessary to put boundaries in place that change your relationship. Even when you choose to forgive someone, you do not have to restore the relationship exactly as it was, or at all.

Other things add to the confusion about forgiving and reconciling. One is the assumption that forgiveness is a preliminary step for reconciliation, where one person says they're sorry, the other one forgives, and they're reconciled. The trouble is that some people say they're sorry because there's pressure to end the conflict. They go through the motions without addressing the real issues. For others, saying sorry is simply an easy way to bring about reconciliation. These kinds of saying sorry are hollow.

Some people make the connection between forgiveness and reconciliation as they were taught as children to end conflict by saying sorry. Most likely they were also taught to reconcile, whether or not either party meant it. At one time, they probably sensed a disconnect between what they were feeling and what they were told to do, but learned to ignore it. As adults, this disconnect lingers, adding to the confusion of what it means to forgive and to reconcile.

Without meaningful forgiveness, reconciliation is thwarted. All too often, two people appear to be reconciled, yet continue to harbour resentments. When they "make nice" and put up with the situation without actually doing the work of forgiving, they become stuck. Worse, rather than deal with the issues, they give up. Sadly, when you say you're sorry, or when you say you forgive, for the sole purpose of reconciliation, you miss the opportunity to work through the underlying issues. Moving to reconciliation too quickly without addressing the issues can make things worse. Without doing the forgiveness work, you may prevent the kind of full reconciliation you wish to achieve.

The Many Faces of Reconciliation

In the best-case scenario, reconciliation follows from mutual work on the problems in the relationship and the issues requiring forgiveness.

There's a world of difference between full reconciliation and going through the motions. Sometimes people reconcile because it is expedient: for the sake of the family, for example. Sometimes it looks like they've reconciled, but they've lost trust in the other person. When one person buries the pain, or feels threatened, diminished, or fearful, this indicates that reconciliation has not happened. We see this in our work with couples who say they got back together, but nothing changed. Understanding these faces of reconciliation has a bearing on forgiveness and your well-being.

Real Reconciliation

Full and healthy or real reconciliation requires that both individuals be willing to address issues; and with forgiveness, the relationship is restored. In fact, it may become even better, as all issues have been addressed. This allows someone to recommit to the person who hurt them. When that happens, real reconciliation, like forgiveness, brings peace and a sense of freedom for both parties. Both are freed from worry about whom to avoid, what not to say, or what not to bring up in conversation. At the same time, this does not mean either of them denies or forgets what happened.

Real reconciliation is based on shared personal truth and the feeling that the other person values their point of view. A sign of real reconciliation is when the person reconciles with the person as they are now, not as they could have been, or should have been. Both parties have learned and moved forward. Even though they no longer relate in the same way they did before whatever happened, the painful occurrence has been addressed and becomes history. When either one is not able to do this, they limit their ability to bring about a real reconciliation. Real reconciliation occurs when both individuals feel they've been heard and understood by the other. When this happens, the problem, which has been addressed, brings them closer together. In our experience, people are able to reconcile to the degree they are able and willing to speak honestly about the real issues in the relationship.

Skin-deep Reconciliation

Unfortunately, sometimes reconciliation takes place solely on the surface, and sometimes the individuals are unaware that they have not addressed the issues. The danger is a skin-deep reconciliation, which comes with a cost: it gives the impression that all is well, but it hides bitterness, anger, or resentment. It also hampers forgiveness when the person denies their experience and betrays their own feelings. They may not be aware how much energy this takes until they're surprised at how angry they still are. This may not pose an immediate problem, but over time, this denial erodes the relationship until it collapses. Some marriages also pay the price as, over time, they fall apart because of skin-deep reconciliations.

There is another kind of passive skin-deep reconciliation where the reconciliation takes place, not by talking about the issue, but through actions. Here, the person shows that they're sorry by benevolent actions such as bringing flowers or making a favourite meal, but cannot, or will not, apologize or even discuss what happened. As a result, the relationship continues, but there is an elephant in the room. Both parties remember what happened, yet avoid dealing with the issue. If this approach is used too frequently, the relationship dries up; it becomes restricted as both people tiptoe around painful issues. Even though this behaviour works well in some situations, the risk is that problems remain unaddressed.

Faux Reconciliation

A faux reconciliation is done intentionally: for the sake of appearances, one or both people involved pretend to be reconciled. Sometimes this is based on a mutual decision not to go there. The problem with passive decisions is that you don't do anything to address the underlying problem. Either one of you may be unable, or unwilling, to address the issue. It is a false reconciliation because the problem remains: nothing has changed and none of the issues have been addressed. This can also happen when one or both parties are forced to reconcile, perhaps for the sake of the family. This only serves to increase the tension caused by outside pressure. The people involved are left struggling, and the relationship is wounded as well.

When conflict happens in a relationship, if you don't address what's hurting, you may find yourself thinking or saying nasty things about the other person as the initial cause festers below the surface. Over time, you risk becoming sensitive about things not even remotely connected to the issue, so that instead of making your life better, faux reconciliation makes it worse.

These faux reconciliations often take place in relationships that are less personal; for example, at work or in social situations. Out of necessity, you go through the motions in an effort to reduce tensions. But this, too, comes at a cost. Because the underlying problem has not been addressed, others may see you as bitter because you harbour resentment or anger that affects your work or social interactions.

Reconciliation in Absentia

Reconciliation where both parties participate is not always possible. This happens when they are separated by distance, by a disease such as dementia, or by death. In these circumstances, in order to restore the relationship, you make a choice to bring about forgiveness and reconciliation in ways that make sense to you and at the same time honour the relationship. For example, an estranged son or daughter may want to honour their parent and their relationship after their parent dies, so they make a special visit to the grave, visit a mutual relative, or do volunteer work in their parent's memory.

There are times when the separation of the people involved is deliberate. In this case, the choice not to make contact is done out of consideration, for fear that contact will cause the other person more suffering. Twelve Step programs put this into practice in their instructions: not to contact the person they have harmed if that would cause more suffering or harm that person in any way.

Frank's Story: "A Lingering Doubt"

I worked in a small office where everyone knew each other. As the space was open, rather than have meetings, we had conversations when we needed them. One day I was surprised to discover that some cash on my desk was gone. I wasn't really worried, but when I asked around, no one knew what had happened to the money.

Sometime later, Sherry asked to speak privately. Sherry told me she thought the money was office money used to buy coffee, which she hadn't had a chance to purchase yet. Sherry paid me back and asked me to keep this between us.

I accepted Sherry's explanation even though, under the circumstances, it seemed odd. I found myself wondering why she hadn't spoken up right away, and why she hadn't checked with me before taking the money.

I thought I had dealt with and forgiven Sherry's "misunderstanding." The problem was I continued to have doubts; why did Sherry need this to be kept private? Without meaning to, I made a mental note to self about Sherry.

At work, everything appeared to be normal; I continued to work with Sherry and saw her in some work-related socializing. However, when Sherry asked me to give her a reference, I didn't feel comfortable. I thought I was doing what was best for her by suggesting that she ask someone else to provide the reference. Sherry became openly hostile. She accused me of being prejudiced. Life at work got worse, not for Sherry, but for me!

You may wonder if Frank did in fact forgive Sherry, or if they actually reconciled after the money went missing. Frank thought he had forgiven her. He considered the matter closed, inasmuch as it affected the two of them. However, when Sherry asked for a job reference, Frank told the truth: he was uncomfortable doing this. Even though he had given her the benefit of the doubt, he honestly didn't think he could give the kind of reference Sherry wanted.

For Frank, the knowledge that you can forgive someone and at the same time put appropriate boundaries in place helped him act according to his conscience. Even though he had reconciled with Sherry, their relationship had changed. Frank was honest with her and let her know it would be better to ask someone else for a reference.

Thinking back, Frank regretted having accepted Sherry's explanation about the money without addressing his doubts. He also regretted Sherry's request to keep the matter secret in what had been a work environment of open discussion and trust.

Is It Worth the Effort to Reconcile?

You may wonder, is it worth it? After all, reconciliation takes time and hard work. In long-term relationships, the history and quality of the relationship impacts your willingness to be forgiving, and ultimately to reconcile. Even though love and commitment increase the desire to reconcile, there are limits. So much depends upon the nature of the friendship or kind of relationship, as well as the willingness of the individuals.

It's as if each relationship has its own bank account; you put positive energy in the relational bank that you can draw on in tough times. This bank has limits. Over time, relationships without savings gradually disintegrate, to the point that there is nothing left to deal with even minor hurts.

What If You Don't Want to Reconcile?

You can have all kinds of reasons for not wanting to reconcile. A real reconciliation is next to impossible with a person who does not acknowledge your feelings or your experience. How do you reconcile if, time after time, nothing has changed? What if the person who hurt you doesn't want to address the issue? What if they can't? What if your safety is at risk? How do you know when enough is enough in a relationship? In part, it depends on how much you value the other person and the relationship. You will work harder and longer for a relationship you care about. However, there are thresholds in relationships; when that threshold is crossed, the issue needs to be dealt with.

What If You Are Afraid to Reconcile?

Some relationships are destructive or dangerous. For whatever reason, such as personal safety issues, you can forgive and choose not to reconcile. Even as you forgive, give yourself the freedom to terminate the relationship if you are at risk. Some relationships are so toxic that no amount of effort on your part will make the relationship healthy.

If you're afraid, look at necessary restrictions to put in place. For example, the spouse who has been abused demands that their partner seek professional counselling before talking about reconciliation. Another example, a very difficult one, is the adult who suffered abuse as a child; after working to address their pain, they may make the choice to forgive for their own peace of mind and choose not to have any relationship whatsoever with the abuser. Their decision not to reconcile comes from strength.

Gaining Understanding

Let's look at the faces of reconciliation using Helen's story from Chapter 1. After a long time and with hard work, Helen experienced many of the different faces of reconciliation before she reconciled with her ex-husband. She describes their faux reconciliation before they divorced, where deeper, more troubling issues were not addressed, not even in therapy.

It is common to bury problems for the "good of the children," yet end up shortchanging the relationship. Helen's faux reconciliation happened as she and her husband decided "not to go there." Finally, Helen says she "Could forgive him, not her [Hazel]," which helped her "meet him in the future without stress." Helen talks about the ease in "our exchange of words." Although there has been a skin-deep reconciliation between Helen and her ex, where they can speak and appreciate each other, their relationship is still strained after the divorce.

Helen was not able to reconcile with the woman who had been her best friend and now was the wife of Helen's ex-husband. For Helen, the years spent with her husband and the fact that he was the father of their children outweighed her friendship with the other woman, who she once said was her soulmate. At the time Helen shared her story, she and her "ex-best friend" had experienced both a faux and skin-deep reconciliation, which were necessary to help Helen get to the point where she could be in the same room with Hazel.

Forgiveness demands that you look below the surface. It's easier to see when others are "wrong" and criticize their assumptions and expectations than it is to look at your own thinking. Helen's hard work brought a sense of peace, reflected in her saying she has become a "better person for having loved and sharing life for the last 24 years." Helen has come to terms with some of her anger, her hurt, and her part in the dissolution of her marriage. The danger in quick and easy solutions is twofold: losing touch with how to do the hard work and avoiding the opportunity to learn from the experience.

When you understand that struggling is part of the process, you can ask yourself: Have I gained understanding? Am I more in touch with my anger or my disappointment? Have I acted with integrity? Asking questions like these helps give you markers along the way. Even if you can't forgive right now, you may be able to avoid lashing out in anger, or suffering debilitating depression, which might be what happened in the past. Doing forgiveness work helps you develop a more balanced approach to successfully handling life's messy details.

4

Living Actively
and Freely through Choice

Thankfully, we have many extraordinary examples of men and women who are not only able to forgive, but they inspire others. Take, for instance, world spiritual leaders such as the Dalai Lama, Pope John Paul II, and Archbishop Emeritus Desmond Tutu. The Dalai Lama has endured many difficult events in his life. For others, it would have been understandable to become bitter or vengeful after fleeing their homeland. The Dalai Lama is neither. He continues to speak about the potential for good in others.

John Paul II demonstrated peace and forgiveness to his would-be assassin, Mehmet Ali Agca. John Paul's meeting with Agca after recovering from his wounds serves as a model. But, even with forgiving, there are consequences. After their meeting, Agca went back to prison to serve out his term, and the Pope's injuries likely continued to impact him.

Archbishop Emeritus Tutu is a Nobel Prize Laureate whose dedication and leadership are the basis for the Desmond Tutu Peace Foundation, which helps individuals and countries engage in conversations about peace, equality, and forgiveness.

It may seem possible for spiritual leaders to forgive, but what about everyone else? We cannot emphasize this enough: forgiving is freeing; a lack of forgiving becomes self-destructive. Those who can't or won't forgive not only miss out, they actually bring harm to themselves. Bitterness saps their ability to enjoy life. Over time, they become angry people. Their anger lies just below the surface, a ticking time bomb easily triggered by seemingly unrelated events. Others are consumed with an inner rage that can lead to isolation and depression.

Some people manage to bury what happened so that to all appearances, they are well adjusted. They get along until something triggers them: then they go ballistic when they encounter a situation similar to the one that hurt them. This overreaction comes as a surprise, even to them. Everyone wonders where all that anger came from. They do not understand that being unable to address underlying issues eats away at them to such a degree that it affects their health. They do not make the connection that burying painful incidents is the underlying cause of their overreaction, anger, or anxiety.

A number of the people we have talked to or worked with were able to forgive even though they suffered traumatic loss. We share stories of people who have forgiven incredible hurt because their stories give us hope. One time, a man approached us during a break in a workshop. He wanted to speak to us privately, to share what happened to him. He did not want to talk even in the small-group sessions. He told us about the death of his teenage daughter. She had been killed by a drunk driver who swerved into a group of people at a bus stop. She had been standing there waiting to go to work.

He said losing her was all the more painful, almost unbearable, because she was so full of life and promise. She had just finished high school and was so excited about going to university in the fall. He mentioned how hard she had worked to get there. Her senseless death was all the more terrible because she had told him how excited she was that her life was beginning to open up.

It had taken him a long time – endless nights, the agony of getting through the trial – to get to a place where he thought he was able to forgive the man who killed her. As a religious person, he wanted to forgive. There were times he thought he had come to a place of peace, and then, wham, he seemed to be right back where he started.

He wouldn't have said it the same way before, but now, after the workshop, he could see that he was still grieving. He grieved not just her death; he grieved the loss of unfulfilled dreams. It wasn't just his daughter's dreams he grieved; he grieved his own. He would never see her finish her education, never walk her down the aisle. He would never be a grandfather.

He and the drunk driver both had to live with the devastating loss, each in their own way. He heard the driver speak in court; he knew the man bitterly regretted he had been drinking. He wished more than anything he could bring the young woman back. He said he often wished it had been him who had died. The man at our workshop wanted us to know that something clicked for him when he heard that even when forgiveness takes place, everyone involved has to live with devastating consequences.

Now that You Know, Make an Informed Choice

One of the most important steps in forgiving seems to be simple: make the choice to begin the process. This is different from "wanting" to forgive. You bring more options and gain strength when you make the effort to see what might impede your decision. By using the Tools and Strategies, by writing your story, by working with the questions about your assumptions and expectations, and so on, you discover possible threats to doing what you want. Many people experience relief simply by making this decision.

Even if you decide to forgive, it doesn't mean you automatically forgive. You need time to work on the complexity of the issue, process your feelings, and look at internalized beliefs that keep you from forgiving.

The crux of this process involves giving you what you need to make choices. Your subsequent forgiveness actions flow from these choices. You can't make informed choices without the necessary information.

Although this might seem simple, knowing you have the ability to choose is powerful. At this point, if you continue to worry that forgiveness is impossible or unwise, we ask you to keep an open mind. Even though you may not realize it, you're the one who determines what it takes to forgive. We offer Tools and Strategies so you are not overwhelmed or at the mercy of your thoughts or feelings.

Living Fully through Choice

You have the ability to reinterpret the events of your life. You have the opportunity to impact your thoughts and feelings by how you perceive and interpret any given event in your life. Living this way is active living.

Feelings, in part, come from our interpretations of events and the kind of language we use. We will talk more about this later. Understanding this idea helps you choose your feelings. For example, you can make a conscious decision to look for the positive and not to dwell entirely on negatives. Culture also plays a role in influencing how we perceive reality and how we make choices. Many of these choices are unconscious ones; these are unthinking choices because we do what's expected. Sometimes what we think of as givens in life reflect unconscious choices. It's easier to see what you always thought of as a given when you travel to countries that have different cultural norms and practices. Sometimes you discover that what you thought of as the only way to do certain things is just one way. You discover that what's acceptable, what seems to be a hard and fast rule, for behaving in one country is not acceptable in another. Seeing other ways to view the world frees you to look deeper at any unexamined choices.

Even though other people affect your feelings, they do not determine them. You have power; you can decide to reframe a particular event in your mind. When you rethink the event, you can change your feelings. Many techniques and practices can help; for example, meditation helps calm the body and the mind. Prayer, contemplation, and reflection bring understanding and wisdom that strengthen your awareness of control over your feelings. Physical exercise also enhances a sense of well-being as the body releases endorphins. Find which of these practices work best for you to build up your sense of well-being and sense of control in your life.

In terms of forgiving, there are times when you think the only choice is that the other person should act first. The point is that you have a choice regardless of how they act. But if your actions depend on someone else's actions, you lose. If you need the other person to do something (i.e., apologize or show you that they feel guilty), you give up power because the other person is in control. It may feel like you're in control, but you have given up control of your forgiving process to the other person.

Choices that Bring Life

Decide to own the process. Resist the temptation to limit yourself with blanket statements such as "You can't trust people in authority." Don't get stuck putting yourself down, saying, "Why don't I ever learn? Why is it always me who gets hurt?" The crux of you being able to forgive is based on understanding the role of choice and developing your ability to make choices by using the Tools and Strategies. These look simple at first glance, and in a sense, they are. Like many things, though, once you know what to do, what seems easy can have a profound effect.

You can choose to forgive, or you can choose to remain stuck with your bitterness, anger, or feeling hurt. Knowing you can do something – and knowing what steps to take – gives you a sense of empowerment to move beyond barely getting by. You can choose to remain a victim, or you can choose to be a survivor and ultimately thrive. Now you have the information you need to make the change you want.

The Flip Side of Making a Choice

Once you've made the choice to forgive, you may be faced with how to handle a loss. Part of the process of forgiving involves grieving a loss, and this is where some of the anguish and struggle lie. The loss and associated grief as part of forgiving are rarely understood. It's easy to concentrate on your pain or anger and disregard the fact that you're grieving. You might not even know exactly what your loss was. It could be the loss, not just of someone you love, but also of a significant relationship. When you divorce, you lose the one you married, and you lose your marriage. It could be you lost faith in a trusted person and, by extension, you lose faith in others as well. If you were hurt by a group of people, such as by a church or an educational institution, you may become cut off as you lose trust in other groups as well. Whether your loss is a person, a group, or your church, you have to grieve the role that loss played in your life.

As we saw in Tool/Strategy 1, you must ground your forgiveness work in respect. This includes respecting your experience of grief over this kind of loss. This acknowledges that your loss is personal; no one else knows how the loss has affected you. It also means acknowledging that your grieving process is affected by your past experience, and your past hurts affect how you react to new ones. No one should tell you, "Get over it." They have no way of knowing how deeply you were hurt and how this impacts your life.

Because there's no one-size-fits-all approach, the differences in grieving for men and women can be a source of additional pain for couples. Sometimes the problem stems from the order in which things happen. Some men, for example, often seem to want to "do something" or "fix it" as a way to deal with loss. Women, on the other hand, may need to talk or actively engage in grieving before they can forgive or reconcile. These differences add to the confusion and hurt. Regardless of the differences for a couple, much depends on the nature of the loss each of them is grieving, and how deeply each one experienced that loss.

T/S 5: SET PERSONAL BOUNDARIES

It's impossible to talk about forgiveness without talking about boundaries. Boundaries are like unspoken ground rules that define how the individuals interact and the relationship itself. Recognizing that the other person has equally valid but different personal boundaries is a necessary part of healthy relationships. In any given relationship, you may not be aware of, or have the same expectations for, boundaries; that's why there's a substantial risk for someone to be hurt. In terms of forgiving, the ability to assess your boundaries helps you decide what's your stuff and what's their stuff in the conflict.

Let's look at a situation to shed light on this: Imagine sitting down at a restaurant next to a complete stranger. Within a few minutes, you know their whole life story, and all their problems. You may feel ill at ease because the stranger has no boundaries and shows no regard for yours. Perhaps you're resentful, because you're captive and forced to listen. You may also feel manipulated by the stranger's laying it all out there, and feel trapped having to respond to needy behaviour.

When Your Boundaries Are Violated and "It's All up to You" Is Taken to the Extreme

In certain instances, when people are in conflict, there's a danger that one of them bears all the responsibility, even though others have their fair share of the blame. Let's look at this family scenario: Donna has organized a family party for her parents' anniversary. Other family members, including Donna's two sisters, accused her of hijacking the planning of family events. Donna wondered if this was true, but thinks, if she didn't do it, would anything get done? Later on, another family member told Donna that the person who first accused her is a constant complainer who always blames others. Knowing this helped Donna let go. As part of Donna's moving forward without bitterness, she made a mental note to ask others to help with future events.

The danger is in getting stuck in "it's all about me" or "poor me; what's been done to me" without considering the actions of the others who are involved. A further danger when you're frequently hurt is that you come to expect to be hurt again. Your expectations change and you begin to doubt yourself, your self-worth, and your abilities. Whatever happened in the past might not in fact have been about you, but the pain is still yours, and you must address it so it doesn't diminish you.

This can also happen in the workplace – for example, when you're passed over for a promotion. It's understandable to take it personally and begin to doubt yourself. When the job goes to someone else, however, the reason may have nothing to do with you. If you get stuck in "me," you won't be able to see other factors, such as the employer's focus on achieving a gender-balanced work environment. In conflicts, looking at the big picture, looking beyond "me," where you're caught in self-doubt, not only prevents you from becoming depressed or bitter, it allows you to make clear-minded decisions.

Glenda's Story: "My Boss Treated Me Like Dirt"

I was upset – very upset – with my boss. Day after day, he treated me with cutting and open disdain. Even though I thought, He's a jerk, at the same time I wondered, What did I ever do to deserve this? It bothered me that my thoughts started to dwell on him. It got to the point that I became fixated. I asked everyone at work, "What am I doing wrong? Is it just me? Please tell me!"

Gradually I lost confidence and began to doubt my own ability. I used to be good at my job. Now, I was a wreck, so my work suffered and then it affected my relationships at work.

The thing was, later I found out what was going on. A work friend told me to forget about what happened. "What good will it do?" she asked. The sad truth was my boss was under the gun at work and at home; one of his kids had some kind of serious illness.

My friend wondered if my boss lashed out and took it out on me because the company was under threat of bankruptcy. At first, I didn't know what I wanted: an apology? A new boss? It felt easier being mad at him than feeling like an idiot or a doormat. Now I see that what I really want to do is figure out why I put up with it or thought it was my fault. I want to make sure I don't let someone else treat me that way again, ever.

Even though Glenda was hurt and angry; it helped her to stop obsessing when she became aware of the bigger picture. She had more information and was able to stop looking solely for her part in the mess.

Look at the Whole Situation

Stepping back to look at the situation allows you to look for all the factors involved, including recognizing boundary issues and recognizing differences between personal relationships and professional ones.

When it becomes all about you, this may be a sign that you're taking responsibility for someone else's behaviour, even when you had no input.

You help move forward by asking: What's the lesson here? What did I learn? Did I trust too much? Did I have my own agenda? Perhaps there was a misunderstanding? Asking these kinds of questions helps you sort through forgiveness issues related to conflict. Asking these kinds of questions leads to valuable insights that will serve you well.

When Are You Willing to Let Go?

We focus on letting go because it's so much better for you to let go and forgive. It is better to learn from your experience and move forward with your life. By letting go, we're absolutely not talking about forgetting what happened, or about not holding the other person accountable, or about disregarding your boundaries. If these things happen, likely you'll be stuck with your pain, anger, and grief, even if you can't see it. Sometimes it takes someone else to tell you that you need to move on because whatever happened is consuming you.

It's entirely different when friends tell you, "You need to forgive and get past this," compared to someone saying, "Just get over it. Deal with it." The first advice is offered as support because they care; the second kind is not offered but stated, and as a result feels dismissive. Being told to just "get over it" implies it's easy to get over whatever happened, which is simply not true. The person giving this kind of advice may have an inability, even an unwillingness, to deal with any kind of pain, whether it's yours or theirs. They might have an agenda, as this approach makes things easier for them. Often, they've also overstepped a boundary; it shouldn't be a surprise that it doesn't feel supportive.

What Prevents You from Letting Go?

Part of becoming free means being able to deal with your triggers. Triggers are personal issues that lie buried below the surface. You may not be aware of all the soft spots that push your buttons. Triggers can have a significant impact on how you respond in new situations based on past hurts. Take, for example, people who can't handle criticism so they avoid taking initiative. They lose the opportunity to learn from valuable feedback and they limit their opportunities.

We all have personal triggers. First, you have to acknowledge your triggers both in terms of your relationships and for forgiveness situations. When you're unaware of your triggers, you're most vulnerable. When triggered, you perceive things in a way that distorts reality. As a result, you falsely link past events with present ones. This happens, for example, to divorced people who vow never to marry again. As they can't trust, they are prevented from even imagining meeting someone wonderful.

Some of the deep-seated triggers mask what's really going on, to the detriment of the person who isn't aware this is what's happening. Stan, for example, asked Alicia to a concert, and she said no. Although this was entirely innocent, for Stan, it was a trigger. As result, he decided not to ask her out again. It reminded him, or triggered for him, how he had been hurt in the past. If this is Stan's pattern (his usual behaviour), he may have deeper issues to address. He may have experienced, for example, feeling rejected as a child or as a teen. If he doesn't look at why Alicia's simply saying no automatically changes his behaviour, he will continue to be controlled by negative triggers.

T/S 6: NEUTRALIZE PAINFUL MEMORIES

Far too often, people are told to forgive and forget. Even if you wanted to, how would you do that? We know you can't really forgive unless you address the issues. We also know you can't forget; if you do, all you do is bury the problem to deal with at a later date, often not of your choosing. Keeping your painful memories buried requires a lot of energy. Understandably, there are circumstances where people would like to or need to forget what happened. Sometimes when the pain is too great, forgetting happens of its own accord. What happened is buried so deeply that it's blanked out. In this case, the way forward is to seek professional help when you're ready.

As a way to handle painful memories, we suggest you "re-member" them. You re-member by breaking your story into manageable parts. You benefit as you consciously re-member, because you connect and reclaim all the parts of your experience, including painful ones, without judgment. You do this in your own time and in your own way as you write what happened (T/S 2). You can also re-member as you share your story in your own way in a safe environment (T/S 3). If needed, get professional help to do this.

If you've tried forgetting as a way to deal with painful memories, you'll know first-hand that it disconnects you from your experience so you can't learn and you can't move forward in a meaningful way. When you re-member, you look at all the issues related to the painful memory, which in turn allows you to find ways to address them, and as a result you're more able to forgive. Finally, this allows you to integrate what happened so you're able to move on with your life. More than that, when you re-member, and you're able to integrate memories about the painful event, you're able to move beyond being a victim to become a survivor.

Dealing with memories can be hard to bear. Sometimes the act of remembering is so toxic, it revives the original destructiveness of what happened. It takes enormous courage to encounter the person who caused the pain and deal with related memories. This is one reason why it's difficult for victims of aggravated sexual assault (rape) to face perpetrators in court. Seeing the perpetrator not only brings back the feeling of being powerless, it is like having to relive what happened. This raises the fear that the perpetrator still somehow holds the power, some kind of hold over them.

Sadly, for their own self-serving purposes, perpetrators take advantage of the idea that others should forget. Remembering painful memories can also cause damage if the other person flaunts it or uses it like a weapon because nothing's been done. This happens, for example, when a victim of childhood sexual abuse has to face the fact that the abuser remained in a position of power or trust: for example, a teacher, coach, or club leader. The victim's memories are all the more painful because the other person got away with hurting them. For victims, this pain is doubly damaging: not only do they have to endure their painful memories, they must deal with the fear that others might be hurt as well.

Victims risk suffering a second time when they talk about what happened – even more so when they're blamed for what happened, or not believed. The abused person is particularly vulnerable the first time they speak about it (recall T/S 1). Worse, if their story is dismissed entirely, they become more vulnerable to being abused again, as they will feel completely powerless or without value.

No one can demand that you forget what happened; no one has the right to forgive on your behalf for the sake of the family. If a child was sexually abused by someone within the family, for example, other family members cannot forgive the abuser on the child's behalf. The only person who's in a position to forgive is the child who has been abused. There may well be multiple issues the abused child needs or wants to address. Being told to keep quiet sometimes happens when others are caught in unhealthy family dynamics, twisted alliances, unclear expectations, or dysfunctional communication patterns. In these kinds of situations, if the one who seeks outside help is seen as a betrayer, this causes them more suffering.

Sometimes the families try to ignore trauma or painful issues by a collusion of silence. Secrets of this kind distort everything: everyone knows something's wrong, even if they don't know exactly what it is. Worse, they can't talk about it to find out how to make changes. If the secret involves abuse – emotional, physical, or sexual – other siblings feel guilty knowing that their brother or sister was abused while they escaped. They can't even raise the issue for fear of causing greater damage. They're left wondering things like "Why them, not me?"

In cases where one parent could not, or did not, protect their child, that parent suffers enormous guilt. It's also hard for others in the family to grieve what happened and to deal with the pain. How can anyone bring about healthy forgiveness with all the secrets, repression, or efforts to forget or deny what happened in these circumstances?

How to Keep Painful Issues from Ruining Your Life

You need a way to manage painful memories without disregarding your feelings so you are able to live without discomfort. Psychologists use the term "containment" to describe how people keep their feelings and thoughts about an event within "mental fences" rather than let them dominate their life. This is one way painful experiences don't interfere with your perception of other events, including new ones. Containment doesn't mean that you forget painful memories; on the contrary, you're able to be honest about them, and this makes it easier to access insights about what triggers you.

Similarly, when you're able to contain a painful relationship, this doesn't preclude you from having other ones. In fact, in harmful situations, containment allows you to assess a relationship objectively, making it easier to see when it's toxic. In a relationship, the steps you take to prevent further harm are ways to contain it. Even if you've contained a painful event and you've forgiven the other person, this doesn't mean you have to reconcile with the person who hurt you (see Chapter 2).

Containment does not mean appeasement. In a given situation, if you've capitulated by appeasing the other person, it is probable that your giving in hasn't helped you grow as a person. It's likely that you've suffered a kind of loss by giving in. With containment, you become empowered because you operate with insight based on "your truth." This is why learning how to contain your painful memories so that you control the memory, not the other way round, is so helpful. Containment gives you more options and more power to learn, move on, and forgive.

Keep Your Anger Where It Belongs: Containment

It's healthy to take responsibility for your anger. Containing your anger doesn't mean you ignore it or deny it; containing it means you keep it where it belongs. This is not always easy. Because so few children are taught how to understand or how to handle their anger, most adults don't have the skills to deal with it. Many parents tell their children, "Don't you dare get angry with me!" The child learns to suppress their anger rather than express it appropriately. The danger is that those who learn to successfully suppress it develop a built-in chip on their shoulder. Their anger is always there, just below the surface.

In part, anger is difficult to contain because it's a Velcro emotion. Like Velcro, anger sticks things together. This is where the confusion begins: anger clumps emotions together that don't necessarily belong. Sometimes people think they're angry, but really they're experiencing frustration, disappointment, or fear. When you're able to identify these as separate emotions, you're in a better position to deal with them appropriately. This gives you more power to deal with the real issue.

When you can't contain painful memories, you interpret everything through the lens of those memories. These non-contained memories also affect your expectations, which have an impact on new situations you experience. Without containment, you self-protect when it's not necessary, or bury yourself in work to avoid being hurt. With containment, your expectations are not limited by one experience; this gives you more choice and control.

You're in Charge, Not Your Anger

You can't change what you don't understand; that's why it's important to know what anger is, so you're in charge, not the other way around. It helps when you understand that anger is an emotional response to un-realized expectations. Anger comes from situations where you've been hurt. When your expectations related to this situation are legitimate, this is healthy anger and helps you address the issue. If your anger is based on unreal or faulty expectations, this leads to unhealthy anger.

So how does this help in forgiving? In relationships, you begin forgiving by looking within: for example, at your sense of being hurt or betrayed. Begin by looking at your expectations: what you expected to happen. As we'll see, your expectations come from your upbringing, society, religious teachings, culture, and so on. It's by examining your expectations that you begin to see if your expectations are legitimate or flawed.

To see how your expectations affect what you thought was just anger, let's look at Todd's reaction to his wife. Todd and Debbie were at a party with his business associates. Unfortunately, Todd made what he thought was an embarrassing mistake in front of the group. It was bad enough when everyone laughed, he said, but what was worse was that Debbie laughed, too.

Todd didn't react at the party, but in the car, he really let her have it. When Debbie burst into tears, he was confused. She had no idea that laughing would make him so angry; he was often the life of the party, making everyone laugh.

We helped Todd sort through his outburst, asking: was it 'just' anger, or did he feel betrayed? Did he expect Debbie to know she should support him by not laughing, even if it was a funny situation? He admitted he wasn't mad that the others laughed, but Debbie should have known better. He realized it hurt because he expected Debbie to be on his side, so he lashed out because she let him down. It's easier to figure out what's bothering you with people you don't know because you have different expectations.

Pseudo-Containment

Those with pseudo-containment sense there's something wrong. They know there's a painful part of their lives. They think their no-go sore spots are just who they are. It's not that they're in denial; they simply have no insight about underlying reasons for their actions. Let's look at John's experience.

John's Story: "I Was Always Wrong, She Was Always Right"

I had a lot of conflict with my sister growing up; I was always the one who got punished, no matter what the circumstances. Because it was always my fault, I learned it was better just to keep quiet. I learned it was pointless to argue. My sister always won. I learned this so well that now, when I'm involved in a situation of conflict with a woman, even at work, I shut down. I'm afraid of losing it one day.

The problem John faced was that he reacted the same way to conflict as he did when he was a boy. The strategy of shutting down worked for him with his sister when he was young, but was not working now that he was a man. As we've seen, it takes a lot of energy to repress feelings. John found it harder to control his temper. He was on the verge of boiling over far too often, so he avoided any kind of argument. He knew he didn't have the same problem defending himself with men, just women.

It's healthier for John to learn not only to recognize his anger, but to develop appropriate ways to handle it. His repressed childhood anger will no longer extend to other women. As he gets in touch with his frustration, which damages his relationships with women, he is able to contain his anger to the original childhood situation. By doing that, he also resolved some long-standing underlying resentment at his sister. Finally, he may also let go of some anger with his parents for what he thought was unfair treatment growing up. The result is that he feels more in control as an adult.

Stuck in the Past or Can't Get a Grip?

If you're not able to contain a painful event, it dominates your life, including the choices you make and the way you live, even if you don't know this is happening. One example is the person who hates all men or all women after a bad marriage; they extend this experience to everyone, poisoning new relationships and overreacting in new situations before they have a chance.

It's easy to confuse non-containment with denial, because denial mimics non-containment. When you're in denial, you don't admit there's a problem. With non-containment, the painful memories control you, even though you don't know this is happening. In both cases, you have a false sense of comfort because you're not dealing with the underlying issues or the situation.

This is why forgiveness requires truth. Whether you repress or deny an issue, or the issue dominates your life (non-containment), you are not able to address it. When you're able to contain painful events, even though you may be cautious, you won't shut yourself completely off.

The more you understand your triggers and are able to contain painful events, the more power you have. As a result, you live with the benefit of lessons learned based on real-life experience.

Barry's Story: "Our Family Was Robbed by My Mother's Companion"

My mother took care of herself until declining health and early stages of Alzheimer's made changes necessary. My brothers and sisters and I wanted to help her stay in her apartment. As much as we wanted to be with her, this was not possible due to work-loads and career commitments, and not all of us lived close by.

We ended up hiring daily caregivers to provide the care we wanted. Of all the home-care workers, Dorothy was Mother's favourite. She ran errands for Mother and dropped in to visit. Soon, Dorothy was part of the family; when we took Mother out for dinner, we invited Dorothy to join us.

Several months went by before Mother complained she had no money. Regrettably, we didn't pay attention; we thought she had forgotten where she put the money, or what she bought. Later, my brother noticed money disappearing. It crossed our minds that one of her caregivers kept the loose change. Because good caregivers were hard to find, we all agreed not to pursue the matter. Sometime later, in an effort to appease Mother, my sister reviewed Mother's bank account. She was shocked to discover 20 checks made out to Dorothy. The signatures on the checks clearly were not Mother's. We fired Dorothy and informed the police. We learned that over $6,000 was missing, not counting the missing loose cash.

We were confused and angry. Before we hired Dorothy, my sister carefully reviewed her references. We felt Dorothy betrayed our mother and our family's friendship. We felt betrayed by a system that allowed Dorothy to take advantage of the elderly. After Dorothy was charged by the police, we learned she had been previously discharged from employers for suspicious behaviour.

Even though it was known in the community, nobody told us that Dorothy had lost other jobs due to her gambling problem. No one had pressed charges against her, so she never faced the consequences. It took two years for the case to go to court. In the meantime, Dorothy got a job in the laundry at a local seniors' residence. Our worst fears were realized; Dorothy continued to have access to vulnerable people.

We went to court to ensure that her criminal record would be available to anyone who planned to hire her. Dorothy pleaded guilty and was given nine months in jail, but was released after three months. Later, this story was published in the local paper. No one in the community said anything to anyone in our family.

If Dorothy were to ask for forgiveness, I would certainly say yes, I forgive. Now there is a sense of acceptance of what happened. I was grateful for the time she spent with my mother. What really hurt was that I felt sorry for my mother; she felt betrayed by the person she thought was a friend. I pity Dorothy; she had our gratitude and respect, as well as friendship with my mother, but she threw it all away to gamble and buy lotto tickets.

I felt a wave of anger when I later saw Dorothy in a hospital waiting room. I felt angry because she ignored me, not even attempting to apologize or explain. At first, I interpreted this as contempt or disregard for Mother. Rationally, I know she's not a bad person, and I understand the power of addiction. However, I still feel guilty for dismissing my mother's complaints about money. I'm also angry that Dorothy tricked my family.

Then Comes Understanding

To help understand, let's look at examples of containment in Barry's story. Barry contained his wave of anger, so he didn't overreact when he saw Dorothy later. He contained it in that he didn't think other home-care workers were untrustworthy. He contained his experience, saying that he no longer dwells on what happened.

Because he contained his feelings, he was able to share his story without bitterness; this allowed him to share in the hope that others would learn from his mistakes. He didn't blame what happened on the system. Even though it made him sad, he didn't dwell on the fact that others who knew about Dorothy didn't warn the family.

In terms of forgiving, Barry grieved the loss in the sense that Dorothy didn't care about his mother or his family as he thought she did. Barry forgave Dorothy, but he was frustrated that everything the family went through wouldn't prevent her from doing the same thing to others.

T/S 7: USE COOLING COMMUNICATION WITH NEUTRAL, NON-LABELLING LANGUAGE

We developed cooling communication to help clients talk about their experience without adding fuel to situations that were already inflamed. Words have power; they cause damage in unseen and unrecognized ways, or bring comfort and initiate healing. Communicating with Neutral Language (CNL) is the intentional use of non-blaming, nonjudgmental words. It helps you engage a rational, more emotionally neutral zone. It helps free you so you don't remain trapped by past events or hooked by emotions. It helps temper extreme emotions with the result that you move through blockages.

We want to stress that you are in charge; using CNL is for your benefit. It helps bring objectivity and clarity to the situation so you see things in a new way. By using neutral, non-labelling language, you can talk and write about your experiences in an honest, yet respectful way (T/S 1). This helps you *contain* your feelings and past events as your choice of words directly impacts how you and others interpret events. It helps prevent you from blaming others. As a result, you have more options to resolve the situation.

CNL changes the dynamics for listeners as well. It opens doors for constructive dialogue. It allows listeners to come to their own conclusions about what happened, as they're not manipulated or influenced by inflammatory words that label or demonize others. It provides listeners with a neutral space to hear without being caught in raw emotional tones. It avoids expressions that put the other person on the defensive rather than listening and considering their position.

At first, using CNL may seem artificial or distant from what you're feeling. With anything new, it takes time. It's understandable if you struggle, if you resist talking or writing in a new way. This is natural: some find it's easier to repress feelings, while others find it easier to vent them. If you remain blocked, you're locked in, so you can't see things any other way. You also want listeners to see it the way you do, and will become angry or frustrated by those trying to help. If you spent years talking about the "rotten jerk" or the "tramp who left you," and how much you suffered, it will take time and energy to say, for example, "My ex-spouse and I live separate lives."

T/S 8: REWRITE YOUR STORY USING CNL

You began the forgiving process by telling your story, by writing what happened (T/S 2) as openly and honestly as possible, without self-censoring. Now, you write your story again, this time using CNL: maintaining your truth but without using any judgmental, blaming, or incendiary words. You want to tell your story in a way that gives you a degree of emotional distance for your own purposes.

Write it so that anyone reading it can understand what happened without more background information. Stick to the basic facts: the "who, what, and when" aspects of your story. Deliberately choose words that do not label anyone in a very positive or negative way. For example, saying you were "injured" doesn't imply why or how. It could be something completely accidental or unintentional. Do not write off the person who hurt you by calling them names: stupid, a cow, that jerk, creep, the sneaking skirt chaser, thieving liar, and so on.

When you wrote your story (T/S 2), you accessed a dynamic that is an essential part of your forgiving and healing process. If you struggled to do this, don't worry, it's a good sign. If you find using CNL to be difficult, this too is a good sign. It's more difficult than you might think to write what happened stripped down to the bare bones, with just the facts in as neutral a way as possible, without editorial comments. Once you are done, set aside your CNL story for future use.

What You Gain

Learning to use CNL helps you speak honestly about your experience, but now your focus is moving towards healing. By intentionally using CNL, you neither deny nor repress your pain: instead, you acknowledge it. It keeps you from thinking in self-limiting terms and becoming a permanent victim. It moves you away from the blaming mode, which can be self-destructive. CNL frees up energy that you can use to get closer to being able to forgive and move on. When your focus is on your process of forgiveness, not just the final outcome, you're able to identify and handle your feelings, thoughts, and understanding of the hurtful situation.

Julie's Story: Without CNL

My sister Peggy always was, and always will be, a total control freak. She's older, so she has always been in charge and always gets her way. Our big family split happened after Mom died and, of course, Peggy was in charge. Peggy, the boss, no surprise there, wouldn't let me have the necklace Mom told me I could have when I was little. If it wasn't for Peggy, there wouldn't be a problem, and we wouldn't be fighting. Mother must be rolling over in her grave. This mess is all Peggy's fault.

Julie's Story: With CNL

The big fight started when Mom died. My older sister Peggy is the executor of Mom's will. A family necklace is the reason for the fight between my sister and me and the rest of the family. I tried to explain that Mom told me when I was little that I could have it, but Peggy says she has to follow Mom's will that the necklace go to the eldest daughter, and then to her eldest daughter. She said, it's a family thing. I'm still angry that Mother told me I could have it. My sister should listen. I would never lie.

Using CNL Helps Shifts the Dynamics

CNL helps redirects energy to the issue rather than the people involved. This makes it easier to address the situation calmly. Reading the first story leads to a particular conclusion, which is Julie's side of the story. Every time Julie tells it, the angrier she gets. Her telling it this way leads others to the conclusion that Julie is a victim, as her sister always gets what she wants. When Julie tells it with CNL, it easier to see there's another side. It opens up possibilities for discussion about the issue. It leaves room for continued dialogue and possible reconciliation.

When you are hurt, you tend to focus on the wound rather than on strategies to deal with it. Using CNL helps you create an emotionally neutral environment. This, in turn, gives you more ability to access a greater range of emotions, which helps you understand the forgiveness issues. It helps you bring about closure: as you look at different ways to interpret a situation, other solutions become evident. CNL helps by opening up possibilities and providing other perceptions of the incident, which leads to other previously unthought-of possibilities.

Using CNL in Conversations:
Say What You Mean and What You Need

CNL conversations are honest and clear communications based in respect (T/S 1). You avoid shutting down the conversation with words that trip an emotional response. On the physical level, emotionally loaded words create stress. Stress colours the way you think, and it affects your reactions. Current research shows that for your body, stress is stress, real or perceived, and has a negative impact. Using CNL enables you to foster a healthy response. Perhaps this is similar to what Buddhist teachers refer to as the "wisdom of cooling the flames."

By using CNL, you recognize that you are responsible for your thoughts, feelings, and actions. It helps you focus on your feelings rather than project them onto someone else. This doesn't mean that you need to be vague when you express feelings. If so, you encourage someone else to define your feelings for you. When you say, for example, "I'm upset," this is open to misinterpretation. People say this when they're not sure what they're feeling. Being upset could mean hurt, sad, or disappointed.

You've created another problem if, by using emotionally loaded words, you put others on the defensive, so they're not able to hear what you're saying. Let's look at what happens when you say, "You betrayed me" versus "I felt betrayed." Casting blame and saying, "You betrayed me" puts the other person on the defensive and moves each of you towards greater conflict. You can't communicate effectively if the other person feels their back is against the wall. The other person becomes more entrenched in their position, and each of you becomes more defensive. However, by saying, "I felt betrayed," you leave room for dialogue. You're not blaming; you're sharing how you feel.

Share Your CNL Story

In all likelihood, you wrote the first story (T/S 2) the same way you told it to others. The next step is to share your story again, using CNL. It's preferable to share it with someone who did not hear the first one. You may want to tell them you're trying to talk about what happened in a new way; it might sound a little flat without the usual emotional words.

Your focus here is on sharing in as neutral a way as possible. Pay attention to your feelings as you do this. If you're comfortable, spend time talking with that person about their reaction. Did you miss any elements? What questions did it raise?

Communications: Being Heard and Being Understood

Good communication involves give and take for who's speaking and who's listening. It sounds simple; why, then, do we misunderstand each other so often? As healthy relationships require both skill sets, we'll look at both aspects.

You may have experienced the difference when someone simply hears your words versus the experience of feeling you've been heard. When you're talking, you're probably comfortable when someone says, "I'm not sure I get it." It feels supportive; it shows they're listening, and they're trying to help by letting you know they don't understand. There's no hint that they blame you because the meaning is not clear. It could be the way you said it, or they just don't understand.

It's not the same experience when somebody says, "I know exactly how you're feeling," especially if you're talking about a significant trauma. Unless they went through exactly the same thing, how could they know? Were they really listening? Was this a pat response, or were they just being polite?

If you're the listener, the danger in saying that you know how the other person feels diminishes what they tried to share. Even saying something like "I can only imagine what you are going through" makes an enormous difference. For the listener, it is better to ask for clarification or paraphrase what the person has said as a way to show you're listening.

The Craft of Paraphrasing

Learning how to paraphrase is a powerful skill: it's useful in listening, in relationships, in conflict resolution, for forgiving, and with reconciliation. By paraphrasing, we mean the ability to put into your own words what you've heard, and then checking with the speaker, asking, "Is this what you meant?" By paraphrasing, you demonstrate that you're listening, not that you're necessarily in agreement. By making the effort to paraphrase, you indicate, "I care about what you're saying and I want to understand."

When paraphrasing is done well, the rephrasing conveys the correct meaning for the other person. This gives them a chance to respond, "Yes" or "No, that's not exactly what I mean." This marks the beginning of a more productive dialogue. When someone exaggerates as they paraphrase, they might have an agenda, or they can only see the issue from their point of view. For example, if you tell someone that you feel ignored, and they respond, "Are you saying I *never* pay attention to you?" they've changed the focus from you to them. By paraphrasing and paying attention to exaggerations or angry outbursts, both speaker and listener can clarify issues and recognize each other's issues.

T/S 9: LEARN THE ART OF LISTENING

We call it the art of listening because real listening involves far more than simply trying to understand what was said. By carefully listening with intention, you respect the other person (T/S 1) and show that they're worthy of your time and energy. When the person speaking knows you're trying to understand, they're less defensive and it's easier for both to stay focused on the issues. If they feel you're not listening, this becomes an issue in itself. It's insulting to be ignored. If they feel you're not listening, they may become angry, or shut down.

You indicate that you're actively listening by nodding your head, or, for example, by responding audibly with affirmations like "Uh-huh." As you listen, look at the speaker in a way that indicates your interest. Try not to interrupt, unless you need clarification. On the other hand, if you're speaking, and it appears the other person is not listening, it is better to calmly check by asking questions such as "Am I speaking too quickly?" If you're frustrated and find yourself raising your voice, check to see if you're trying to force the issue. This is when clarification through give and take helps both parties.

Sacred Listening

There are levels of listening. In sacred listening, the listener honours the truth of the other person on all levels: body, mind, and spirit. Sacred listening does not mean blind support, but support based on your commitment to help others build healthy lives and heal souls. This honouring means that you acknowledge and

➤

respect their feelings, and hold these in trust. There's a difference between sacred listening and active listening. In active listening, your focus is directed to receiving information and checking to see you have understood what the other person has said as information. In sacred listening, your focus is respect (T/S 1); as you listen, you demonstrate support for the person, not necessarily for what they've done.

5

The Apology:
Everything You Need to Know

As we've seen, forgiveness and reconciliation are integral parts of personal relationships and social interactions. Being able to apologize plays a critical role in the process. That's why making an apology is considered to be a hallmark of forgiveness. There's more to the apology than the ability to offer one; you also need to know what to do when you're listening and when you accept one. Learning how to handle apologies is a life skill. The problem is that many people haven't developed that skill.

Making effective apologies is hard work; surprisingly, there are not many places to develop the skills to do it well. Despite its importance, the apology is often minimized, and in some cases, misused. Keep in mind that apologies are not all the same; there are as many kinds of apologies as there are people and the situations they encounter. Because we're not perfect, misunderstandings occur even with the best intentions and among the best of friends. In this chapter, we will look at common apology pitfalls and help you learn how to make and receive an apology.

Timing: Knowing When to Apologize

Apologizing immediately after a mishap says something quite different from apologizing much later. At best, an immediate "sorry" signals you recognize the other person's pain, and admit that you're partially responsible for what happened. This works well for minor issues, but with serious ones, apologizing right away suggests you haven't taken the time to think through the issue. It suggests you may not understand the other person's point of view or appreciate what they went through. It's possible that the two of you have different interpretations about what happened. If you apologize without thought, you can't be sure you share the same understanding about what happened or that either person's understanding fits the situation. Without discussion, you risk inadvertently hurting the other person again.

Sometimes the apology is part of a process; it may be necessary to apologize right away, and again later. When the apology feels genuine, this signals openness to further discussion about what happened. The other person may need to hear the apology more than once as they access different levels of their hurtful experience. As the process continues, further discussion allows both parties to understand the nature of the hurt, and what is needed to repair the damaged relationship.

Let's consider this scenario: a husband and wife go to bed angry after a heated argument. The wife is sure her husband is awake even though his back is towards her. She says, "I need to talk." "Enough already"! he replies. "Tell me what you want. I'll say whatever you want."

His saying "I'll say whatever you want" is not an apology. In fact, it makes things worse. He didn't acknowledge that he knows she feels hurt. The tone of his reply maintains the sense of anger without a way for either of them to address it. He doesn't respond to her need to talk; he shuts the process down. She wants to work it out, even though from his perspective, the timing is not the best. It might be better if he suggested that they talk about the issue the next day, saying something like "I'm sorry, but I can't do this now. Let's talk tomorrow."

On the Receiving End: Why Some Apologies Don't Work

It is a misconception that if you can't accept an apology, you're the one with the problem. If problems return after receiving an apology and you're left wondering, "Why can't I forgive?" it may not be evident that what happened triggered more issues than the apology addressed.

Your difficulty could be a problem with the apology itself. Depending on how deeply you were hurt, you may need more time to heal. No matter how good the apology, it won't work if you've forgiven in the past but saw no change in behaviour.

If you are struggling, begin by looking at the reasons why the other person apologized. If you question their sincerity, regardless of the explanation given, you won't be able to accept their apology and you won't want to put yourself in another vulnerable position. The other person has to earn your trust to restore the relationship as it was. If you fear that if you don't accept the apology it will disrupt the relationship, this presents another difficulty. Here, you feel revictimized because you still haven't addressed the underlying issue.

If something was missing in the apology or wasn't right, you might begin to wonder things like "Were they only sorry because they were caught?" Apologies feel hollow when the other person wants to close the issue as quickly as possible without any input from you. It feels like you are in a bind and you have to accept their apology. If you don't, you feel bad. This makes you fear bringing up the issue again, which presents another difficulty. Here, too, you experience a kind of revictimization because you can't address what happened, you can't criticize their apology even though you feel worse, and nothing has been resolved.

The apology also falls flat when the other person is sorry that you're upset, but they think they did nothing wrong. This is why as you listen to their apology, you need to know what's upsetting you and what it is they're sorry for. If by saying "sorry" they're only expressing sympathy, what's missing is a sincere offer to take responsibility for their actions. Even if what happened cannot be changed or repaired, their offer to try to do that as part of their apology is healing. An apology that is offered without an attempt to repair the damage is hollow and insulting. If a narcissist apologizes, the situation is more about them than about you; it is possible they don't really care about the relationship. It's manipulation, not an apology, if the other person's purpose was to get you off their back, or because they got caught.

Perfunctory Apologies: Apologizing without Apologizing

The hurried "sorry" of someone who bumped into you comes from their desire to be polite. At times, this kind of perfunctory apology is the best thing to do. At other times, perfunctory apologies ring hollow: for example, the apology you receive for a company's poor service when they don't do anything to correct the situation.

Blaming Apologies

Apologies also ring hollow when someone apologizes but then says you caused them to act that way; it was your fault. They say, "I'm sorry, but you made me angry when you did this or that, which set me off." They think they've done their bit to restore the relationship, even though they've blamed you. The person is not apologizing; they're processing the issue or justifying their behaviour.

It's also confusing when it appears that someone apologizes, but all they've done is offer sympathy or support. They say things like "I'm sorry you feel that way." It's not an apology, as they haven't taken responsibility for their actions.

It's also not always helpful when someone says, "Let me explain." If you're the one apologizing, ask if an explanation would help. If you're the one receiving an explanation rather than an apology, and it feels like they're trying to justify what they did, it's likely they haven't apologized at all.

What Body Language Says

Whether you are offering or accepting an apology, you gain a lot of information by observing body language, voice tone, and gestures, such as physical distancing. We all react to non-verbal clues, including facial expressions, arm placement, body tenseness, and so on. All of these change the dynamics of the apology for both parties. If your body language or non-verbal gestures don't match what you're saying, you confuse the other person, to the point they won't trust what you've said.

Action Apologies:
When Actions Speak Louder than Words

In some cases, people don't say anything; they apologize through their actions. They make an effort to make it up to you without actually apologizing. Sometimes, for any number of reasons, it could be due to embarrassment or pride; they can't bring themselves to say they're sorry. Other times, they think the action apology works best, as one or both parties can't tolerate the emotional intensity of a spoken apology.

This action apology often works for minor issues, especially when the two people know each other well. It works when both people know this is what's happening, and it's acceptable to the one who was hurt. The danger is when the underlying issue remains unaddressed and unresolved. The person on the receiving end of the apology doesn't know what the person acting out the apology was actually sorry for. Similarly, the person who acts sorry doesn't know if they're on the same page with the person they hurt. Neither of them can be sure if the acted apology will restore the relationship, even if they act as if it has. The one who's been hurt may just be going through the motions that all is better.

The Apology as a Restoration of the Power Balance

Whenever a significant hurt takes place between people, the relationship itself undergoes a shift, which affects the balance of power. An apology helps restore the power balance, so that no one feels vulnerable or humiliated. However, some people fear showing any weakness, or are unwilling to give up their upper hand in the relationship. They resist apologizing because this means acknowledging they did something wrong, which implies weakness.

The one who sincerely wants to reconcile has to apologize in a way that restores the power balance in the relationship. Their apology needs to address the other person's needs, including feelings of vulnerability or shame, and the resulting sense of loss of personal power. It's not up to the offending party to set the agenda to restore the relationship. If they find that the other person's expectations are too difficult, they should seek guidance from someone neutral or find a mediator. Sometimes the person who was deeply hurt wants to get even, triggered by a primitive response to their sense of losing power and their need to restore it.

It's more complicated to restore the balance of power when what happened (the offense) was public but the apology was given in private. For example, when the reputation of the person who was hurt has been damaged, this creates issues that a private apology will not necessarily address. A public apology may be needed to restore the balance of power so that both people feel valued by each other and in a public way, so no one suffers a loss of face or esteem.

When You Offer an Apology: Why and What Are You Trying to Do?

Before you make an apology, especially for more serious matters, take time to look at what it is you hope to achieve: Why do you want to be forgiven? Are you sorry for what you did? Are you uncomfortable because you have hurt someone? Are you apologizing so you feel better? Taking the time helps you sort through your thoughts and emotions. Even if the other person played a part in what happened, you are responsible for the choices you made.

You also need time if either of you feels it would be helpful to discuss what happened before you apologize. If you apologize without any kind of discussion, this shows you recognize their pain, and acknowledge you are at least partially responsible. But if you talk about what happened, the other person has more assurance that you understand what you did and how your actions affected them. By discussing the issue, you both have a chance to speak your truth and address the issues.

Ten Steps to a Successful Apology

1. **Ask to speak to the other person when it's convenient for them.** This demonstrates your seriousness and the sincerity of your intentions. Offer to go to them, or a place they choose, when you apologize. If it's not possible to speak to them, consider writing out your apology. Using email to apologize is acceptable only for minor

infractions. Email is seen as easier and impersonal, so with serious matters it is not effective.

2. **When you meet, try to remain calm.** If you're stressed, seek out a friend for support. Do not drink alcohol or use any other crutch to give you courage. If you're anxious, do what you can: take deep breaths; remind yourself that you can do this. Sometimes admitting to the other person that you're anxious is helpful. If the other person becomes upset, it's not necessarily your fault, as they also have issues. If the other person becomes angry, it's likely they're hurting.

3. **Before you begin your apology, ask the other person to hear you out.** If they have a habit of interrupting, let them know that you need to speak without interruption before they respond. For chronic interrupters, make an agreement that raising your hand in a "stop" position helps let you finish, and is meant to help you apologize.

4. **Resist the temptation to talk about your own hurt, even if you were also hurt.** Even if you have a valid point, the other person is likely to become defensive, so they spend more energy defending themselves rather than hearing what you have to say.

5. **Use "I" statements.** Acknowledge your mistakes. State what you've done or haven't done. When you start sentences with "I," this helps focus on what you take responsibility for. Starting sentences with "you" is interpreted as passing the blame. By talking about the other person's behaviour, you weaken your apology.

6. **Keep your apology focused.** Get to the point. Don't wander off topic. Long-winded explanations are often interpreted as excuses rather than apologies. Try to ensure that the other person hears what you're sorry for and can see that by apologizing, you are taking responsibility for your actions. Let them also take responsibility for their actions.

7. **Listen.** When the other person responds, resist the temptation to interrupt with explanations. Make every effort to demonstrate your interest in what they have to say. Try not to look away or look down. When they have finished speaking, ask appropriate questions. Do

not let anger get in the way, even if you are accused of something inaccurate or unfair. Politely tell the other person that you will resume this discussion another time if either of you becomes too emotional.

8. **Be clear about what action, what issue, you're trying to address.** Check to see if the other person sees the situation differently. If you disagree, offer to take some time so you can think about what they've said. Ask what you can do to repair the damage. Listen carefully. Reassure the person that you are sincere and want to make amends. If you think they are unreasonable, try not to become defensive. If you do feel defensive, explain that you need time to think about how you can make reparations, and you will get back to them.

9. **Do not assume that it is back to business as usual once you've apologized.** If your attempt to apologize wasn't successful, rather than criticizing the other person, examine your apology further. The other person may have residual feelings and may want to talk about it again. Let them; it is part of the healing process, part of their forgiveness process.

10. **Recognize that the person may not accept your apology.** Do not get angry or interpret their refusal as rejection. They may change their mind later, or they may not. Your apology is about taking responsibility for your actions. It is based on your desire to live with integrity, according to your beliefs and values.

Be careful you don't trivialize apologies, either, by overdoing them or by overuse. Doing so sends the message that your apology does not mean very much. People get tired of hearing apologies when there's been nothing to apologize for. When you do have to apologize for serious issues, it is less meaningful.

When You Receive an Apology

When the other person apologizes, they demonstrate that they value you and respect your relationship. When you receive a sincere apology, this helps reduce your stress and releases some of the tension in the damaged relationship. Take the time you need to work out what happened, handle your pain, and deal with resulting stress. The degree of stress you experience corresponds to how significant the relationship is to you and how deeply you were hurt. Recognize that you have to deal with different kinds of loss, including your view of the relationship as it was, or the loss of your sense of power within the relationship. In some cases, you also have to deal with losses such as changes to your sense of identity or self-worth.

It is wise to be skeptical if the other person is annoyed when you don't immediately accept their apology. Their impatience signals that their apology is expedient rather than heartfelt. They want to move on for their own needs rather than yours. If you had a role in what happened, while it's important that you acknowledge this, let the person finish apologizing. Pay attention to what they're apologizing for: are they sorry for their actions that hurt you, or sorry for how you're feeling? If they're sorry that you're hurting, they're offering you sympathy, not necessarily apologizing.

When someone apologizes and you feel worse, or if the apology doesn't sit well, these questions help clarify what you're feeling and what you need in order to forgive: Did the other person focus on their actions, or yours? Did they blame you for what happened? Did they expect you to accept their apology immediately, without any discussion or follow-up? Did they ask, "Is there anything I can do to make it right?"

What Do You Need to Happen?

When you insist that the person who hurt you must apologize before you forgive, you've made their actions a prerequisite for your healing. If you require that they do something before you forgive, you've given away some of your power to the person who hurt you. Regardless of what the other person does or doesn't do, you have the power and the choice to forgive and decide whether you will reconcile.

Intentional versus Non-Intentional Hurts

We may find it hard to accept that we make mistakes. When we're aware of our own ability to mess up, it makes it easier to accept someone else's mistakes. If you have a hard time accepting mistakes, it is likely you'll have a harder time with forgiveness and be less likely to reconcile. You're less likely to feel threatened if you find out that the other person's behaviour was not intentional. You may still be annoyed, but what happened feels less personal. If you think that the other person accidentally hurt you, you don't need to address a power imbalance in the relationship. As there was no harmful intent, it makes forgiveness and reconciliation easier.

When an Explanation is Better Than an Apology

As we've seen, generally speaking, an apology addresses emotional and psychological needs: the person receiving the apology thinks, "I'm being heard; the other person is making an effort to repair the hurt." However, there are times when receiving an explanation is more useful. An explanation tends to be more cerebral because it addresses facts rather than feelings. Sometimes an explanation is appropriate to the particular circumstances, such as when your bill is wrong in a restaurant. Most likely, if you receive a satisfactory explanation, and if the situation is rectified, you'll be satisfied.

There are times when receiving an apology from a business, or an institution like a hospital or university, makes things worse – especially if no steps are offered to rectify the problem. Sometimes all you want is an explanation because it is more useful: for example, finding out why your flight was delayed and how this will be handled. Employees of large businesses sometimes experience a diffusion of responsibility, so they don't feel the same level of concern as if they were personally responsible. For some companies, this is normal business practice. It is unfortunate when these practices erode trust and apologies ring hollow.

Handling Valid Criticisms versus Being Attacked

Valid criticism, depending on the spirit in which it is given, can be extremely useful. Whether you feel attacked depends on the circumstances of the criticism. If you feel belittled or disrespected, or you sense that the other person had a hidden agenda, it's hard not to be defensive.

When someone offers constructive criticism to be helpful, apologies are not necessary unless the way the criticism was offered was hurtful.

You need to learn how to respond appropriately to valid criticism. Just because you're hurting doesn't mean someone intentionally meant to hurt you. For example, if you were told that you are not doing well as part of your work evaluation, your supervisor is responding appropriately to your poor performance. Your boss is giving you their perspective based on specific criteria. While comments about your work are appropriate, your boss should be expected to apologize for derogatory, unprofessional, or personal put-downs.

Being Able to Let Go

When you accept an apology and forgive, you're able to let go. This also allows you to continue to work through the issues at deeper levels. By accepting the apology, you neutralize the situation, which allows both of you to move forward. However, the underlying reasons why and how you let go make all the difference. When you forgive and let go, even as you remember the incident, you're able to put positive energy back into continuing and building the relationship.

Letting go does not mean that you forget what happened or that you're being passive. Making a conscious decision to let go is an active choice that you make for a variety of reasons. Sometimes you let go because you don't believe resolution is possible. You choose your battles, as there are more significant issues at stake or there's nothing to be gained. You can also let go because you're taking the high road, which is better for you as a person.

On the other hand, you can also let go because you realize there's no opportunity to salvage the relationship, such as when the other person is completely unavailable and cannot, or will not, engage in dialogue. In this case, you let go and moved forward without resolving the situation, knowing you've done all you could.

When one person hurts another, they've hurt the relationship as well as the person. Take, for example, this situation: Paul sold his car because his friend Tony told him that he could get a great deal on a car

Paul wanted. Later, Paul found out that Tony sold that car to someone else, who paid more. By doing this, Tony showed how little he valued Paul and the relationship. For Tony, it was all about money. In a sense, Paul was able to cut his losses in the time and energy he would have invested in a shallow relationship.

The Risks in Letting Go

When we talk about letting go, we're not talking about those relationships you have outgrown and no longer wish to maintain. We are referring to relationships you hoped to continue. There are risks in letting go, as nothing is solved and issues get buried. In a relationship, if you let go too often, you risk damaging it. When you let go, you've chosen not to put energy into dealing with the issue, and you've withdrawn energy from the relationship. This kind of cutting yourself off can feel like emotional amputation. Murray Bowen, a well-known family therapist, talked about this kind of cut-off or terminating of a relationship as a way some people handle anxiety: for example, the daughter who moves away from home, thinking a geographic cure will help her get along with her parents. This kind of decision comes with a cost, as the person never learns how to deal with relational conflict.

6

Avoid Detours
and Traps in Forgiving

We know that emotions impact forgiveness, both positively and negatively. We also know that the more you're aware of your experience of feelings and emotions, the healthier you become. The more you understand, the more you're able to make conscious choices about forgiveness and reconciliation. The reverse is true as well: if you're not aware, and have little understanding of feelings and emotions, the more susceptible you are to traps in forgiving.

For our purposes here, we use the term "feelings" in the sense that an individual is consciously aware of their experience of emotion. A healthy adult has the ability to be aware of their feelings; they're able to express their emotions in an appropriate manner where, when, and how they choose. Being able to express your emotions in constructive ways isn't always easy, even for healthy adults. Part of this means that when you experience an emotion, you understand that you do not have to react immediately. As we saw, being able to use techniques such as Communicating with Neutral Language (CNL) gives you insight and control. Being able to express your emotions constructively makes it easier to be truthful, even when it's difficult. When you're not able to do so, this shuts conversations down and sets up barricades in your relationships.

An immature or unhealthy person is either ruled or blocked by their emotions. When they're overwhelmed by their feelings, they express them in destructive ways, harming themselves or others. When they're unaware of their feelings, their anger sits just below the surface. When their anger is blocked, the danger is they deal with this by turning to alcohol or drugs, for example.

T/S 10: RECOGNIZE AND UNDERSTAND
THE EMOTIONAL DIMENSIONS IN FORGIVING

If you struggle with forgiving, it's possible that you're caught at the emotional level. It makes it difficult to sort through issues if you don't know what emotions you are experiencing, or struggle to name them. The more you know about emotions, the more confident you feel that you're in control; your emotions don't control you. We're grateful to the work of many others for their research and insights on emotions. To help identify emotions as you work with forgiving, we use four categories of emotions: achievement, approach, resignation, and antagonistic. Keep in mind that there is no reason to fear, as each emotion serves a useful purpose. No emotion is good or bad in itself.

Achievement emotions include feelings such as joy, pride, elation, and satisfaction. These occur when you have a sense of accomplishment, whether personal or professional. You might experience one of these emotions after a reconciliation, for example. *Approach emotions* occur when you're looking forward to the future: you experience feelings of hope, interest, or surprise. *Resignation emotions* include sadness, fear, shame, or guilt when you suffer a loss, such as the death of a parent, partner, or friend; a significant relationship; a job; or financial losses. Most people find it easy to name *antagonistic emotions*. These include anger, disgust, and contempt. You experience these when you've been harmed morally or physically.

Most often, people struggle with resignation and antagonistic emotions around forgiveness and painful relationships. As examples, we'll look at pride, fear, and guilt.

Pride can have a powerful impact on forgiving and relationships. Pride has two aspects; one is negative, and the other is healthy or positive, related to a sense of accomplishment. Take, for example, the person who takes pride in being an honest person, which is a good thing. However, it is hurtful if they take pride in being honest regardless of who gets hurt. They may say things like "I'm telling you this for your own good." When they make no effort to be respectful, this is thinly masked hostility. Pride is destructive if it means more than the other person or the relationship itself.

When you suffer the loss of a meaningful relationship, this triggers a range of possible emotions, including fear, sadness, shame, and guilt. Any one of these can affect your response and your ability to forgive. Fear holds you back in all kinds of ways, especially in terms of forgiving and relationships. Fear leads to tunnel vision, or can alter your perceptions, both of which make it more difficult to address the issues. Blind fear can cause you to abandon your values or even hurt the people you love. Even when you want to forgive, you can be held back by fear of change. You pay a price: over time, being caught by fear affects your ability to feel and to love. You become emotionally frozen; you shut down; you lose the ability to experience life fully. The problem is not fear itself; the problem stems from acting unconsciously out of anger, for example, rather than addressing the fear.

Guilt, like all emotions, can be healthy or unhealthy. It's a healthy sign if you're uncomfortable betraying your beliefs. Guilt can serve as an alert; this helps by motivating you to apologize and make amends. Problems occur when feelings of guilt are inappropriate; for example, when you feel responsible for whatever happens, even though it is beyond your control. Take, for example, a wife (or husband) who feels ill with overwhelming guilt when the marriage failed despite all her efforts. As she believes all marriages must be maintained regardless of the circumstances, even dangerous ones, she is consumed by guilt. This is unhealthy guilt.

It's not healthy when you feel guilty for not *immediately* forgiving. This guilt is misplaced, because it ignores the fact that forgiveness is a process. It's important to forgive at your own pace, and honour your own truth. Your guilt is misplaced if you think the other person has a right to your forgiveness. When you're not able to forgive, especially when you want to, you may feel a sense of shame. Shame is a kind of internalized victimhood that is hard to deal with because, like fear, it paralyzes you. Guilt becomes toxic when it's accepted without question.

The more you understand the complexities of emotion, and of forgiving, the easier it becomes to have compassion for people who cannot forgive. Having compassion does not mean enabling non-forgiving. It does not mean you become an enabler for those caught in anger, in depression, in being victims, or for those plotting revenge. Neither does having compassion mean that get you run over in your relations with a narcissist or a bully, for example. They both struggle with forgiveness because they don't recognize the needs and rights of others. They have difficulty admitting they did something wrong. Similarly, they don't recognize when they should apologize, or they choose not to. However, when you're in conflict, narcissists and bullies will forgive if it suits their needs.

T/S 11: USE THE HEALING NATURE OF HUMOUR

We agree that laughter is the best medicine. Humour helps break emotional impasses. It helps free relationships when we are able to laugh with friends at painful incidents. When you're able to laugh with the other person, you know that relationship is recovering. It's possible that through your use of humour and working through the issue, your relationship will be stronger.

Many times, the only person who can laugh with you in a painful situation has gone through the same thing. Whether humour is helpful depends on your intentions and the nature of the relationship. Whether humour is appropriate and how the person who was hurt responds depends on the circumstances and how they perceive what you were trying to do.

Humour is powerful; it makes things worse if it is misused and the person feels dismissed, or if what happened is just not funny. In these situations, looking for a funny side seems insensitive, even disrespectful. No one feels like laughing when they've been hurt; all their attention goes to their wound.

When You Need Emotional Distance: Do You Laugh or Cry?

At one workshop we gave, a woman mentioned that she looked forward to attending an upcoming function, adding, "It's no big deal that my ex-husband and his new wife will be there!" When we responded, "The lady doth protest too much," she laughed. "You're right. I just need to look better than the new wife!" Humour helped her see that this was the first time she was comfortable sharing unresolved issues from her divorce.

At times, it's hard to know whether to laugh or cry. We aren't always aware that humour gives us emotional distance from painful events. Getting emotional distance helps us see another perspective. Humour helps us recognize truths we could see in no other way. It helps free us from rigid perspectives that keep us paralyzed.

Humour provides cognitive restructuring that helps you move on and ultimately forgive. Peter shared this story: I was working with a couple who were arguing bitterly. At one point they stopped and looked at me. Not sure exactly how to best respond, I smiled and thanked them for the lively demonstration of how they fight. They were shocked. I recognized as they smiled sheepishly that my remark broke the tension. I was then able to examine with them their argumentative style. Using humour in this way helped the couple take a step back and have a fresh look at their relationship.

T/S 12: ACCESS THE WISDOM OF YOUR BODY, MIND, AND SPIRIT

Bodywork and Physical Exercise

We want to stress how beneficial bodywork and exercise are as part of the forgiving process. If your focus is on the mental, psychological, or spiritual roles, the danger is not paying attention to your body. We've seen that stress directly impacts your health and well-being. In terms of forgiving, painful memories are often retained in the body as tension or inexplicable kinds of pain. Common areas of tension are shoulders, lower back, and the head (headaches). Bodywork helps you access insights about your emotions and what happened to you. For example, if you tense up each time you remember a painful incident, this signals that the issue is not resolved. We often say of people who cause tension that they're "a pain in the neck," or of annoying people that "they're a thorn in my side" because they show the body-emotion connection.

Sometimes you have to go beyond your comfort zone. Some people feel uncomfortable being touched due to personal history, or because of cultural or religious factors. Go slow, respect your body, but don't give up. In terms of bodywork and exercise, choose which suggestions are appropriate to your physical condition and circumstances. Seek out an appropriate level and manner of exercise that works with your body, health, and lifestyle. While it is accepted that exercise is beneficial to us, it is sometimes overlooked that it also helps us get in touch with emotions and painful incidents.

Consider therapeutic massage with a registered massage therapist or a therapist who specializes in bioenergetics. Techniques that incorporate breathing practices also help reduce tension. Yoga, tai chi, and meditation are other ways to bring calm and healing to your body.

Bodywork is not limited to exercise and therapeutic treatments; you also need to eat a proper diet and reduce stimulants. Stimulants, including caffeine, can trigger an anxiety reaction by elevating your heart rate and metabolic levels. Bodywork includes getting enough sleep. Some people think alcohol makes them more relaxed. It doesn't. Worse yet, it provides short-term faux-relaxation and interferes with sleep. It goes without saying that alcohol and tense emotional situations are a bad combination that will not help the forgiving process.

Intuition

If you are intuitive, pay attention to your thoughts, emotions, and body responses. An intuitive person pays attention to non-verbal cues; when these are combined with other information, it helps them understand the situation on another level. It also gives them another perspective, which is helpful in relationships and forgiving.

Guided Imagination, Guided Meditation, and Active Imagination

Mediation, centering, and other techniques are useful as a general practice, not just when you're working through painful issues. While we can't cover all practices, here is a very basic one. Remember that you're in total control of the process.

Begin by going to a private, quiet space to centre yourself. If you're indoors, sit in a comfortable chair. Close your eyes. For the next five minutes, listen for the sounds around you, such as the wind, the rain, or your own breathing. If you find yourself becoming anxious or bored, or your mind is racing, gently bring yourself back to the present moment. If you find yourself flooded with thoughts, let them go. It may take several attempts before this exercise feels comfortable. We encourage you to be patient.

Learning to use active imagination and guided meditation are other effective ways to access your feelings and gain insight into what's holding you back. These techniques are not for everyone. If you are depressed or feeling fragile, we encourage you to work with a therapist to help with feelings that seem threatening or confusing.

Here is a sample of an active imagination exercise focused on forgiving. You need a quiet place where you will not be interrupted.

Take time to relax before you start. Close your eyes. Imagine you're in a safe environment, talking to the person who hurt you. Tell them what you are feeling and what you want them to know. Resist judging your feelings and thoughts at this point; let it flow.

After the imagined experience, write down your thoughts and feelings. Look for emotions. You are trying to unpack your feelings. If this evokes strong feelings, it is a sign that this exercise is touching on something important.

Keep in mind that you are safe: you are not acting on those feelings and thoughts; you are simply gaining access to them. That's it! This can be very difficult. We include this as much for your information as the suggestion that you try it, especially if you experience fear or resistance.

Doing Things You Enjoy

You may not have thought that a hobby, where you spend time doing something you enjoy, provides much-needed respite from negative feelings or personal struggles. Playing a musical instrument, gardening, creative writing, or hiking, for example, is more than helpful – it is restorative for your body, mind, and spirit. This is another way to access wisdom. Art and music also are creative ways for expression when words get in the way. Alternative therapies can lead us to think outside the box and access different personal dimensions.

7

Anger: Who's in Charge: You or Your Anger?

The Gifts and Hidden Costs of Anger

In almost all cases, anger plays a role in forgiveness. It's easy to become bound by anger after being hurt, even when this does you more harm than good. Part of the process of forgiving is looking at whether you are *unwilling* to forgive or *unable* to forgive, and the reasons why.

If you're *unable* to forgive, you may have reasons. If you have been hurt so badly that you don't have the strength or the necessary skills to forgive, you will likely experience a sense of powerlessness. An *unwillingness* to forgive is often based in unresolved anger. What do you want to do with your anger? Do you want to seek revenge or resolve the issues?

It is possible your unwillingness or hesitancy to forgive is based in what you think forgiveness means. Some people and some cultures regard forgiveness as a sign of weakness. For some, seeking revenge is not only their right; it is their duty, no matter the consequences for themselves or others. As we have seen, there is a cost for the person who does not forgive, including negative effects on their health and well-being.

Anger is a Velcro emotion; with all things sticky, it's hard to separate what belongs where. Other emotions, such as fear, hurt, or disappointment, become attached to anger. As we saw in T/S 10, when these emotions are mistaken as anger, it becomes all the more confusing to sort through forgiving issues.

What Is Anger?

Very briefly, for our purposes, we describe anger as a normal human emotion in response to threats or provocation. Those stuck in anger rob themselves of personal growth and opportunities to enjoy life. There is nothing life-giving in anger – it leads to bitterness, depression, isolation, or permanent victimhood.

A helpful way to understand anger in the context of forgiveness is by seeing anger as a response to unrealized expectations (Chapter 2). When you have appropriate expectations that are not realized, this leads to healthy anger. On the other hand, unrealistic or dysfunctional expectations bring about dysfunctional anger. A helpful question to consider in forgiving is "What expectation of mine was not met?" This is challenging, as you may not be aware what your expectations are. If so, your expectations remain unconscious or hidden, and you will find it easy to justify your anger regardless of the circumstances.

Expectations can easily get in the way. Some members of minority groups become hypersensitive to even the hint of discrimination, even when there is none. Their expectation is that others always treat them badly. Therefore, they reason, they have a right to their anger, as they are members of a discriminated group. In extreme cases, their anger prevents them from having any kind of relationship with a person outside of their group.

Processing your anger is empowering. You have choices. Rather than focusing on someone else's behaviour, focus on your expectations. In your relationships, you can clearly identify your expectations to the other person. Let's take a look at what happens when expectations are unclear.

Cheryl's Story: "One Strike and You're Out"

Cheryl was furious when Bill cancelled their date to join friends for a weekend ski trip at the last minute. "I was so angry, I couldn't even listen to the reasons why he couldn't make it this time. I didn't tell him, but I decided, I'm done. He'll never know he just ended what could have been a great relationship."

We explored with Cheryl her anger that led to her extreme reaction, where she acted without thinking. It was unfortunate, especially as Cheryl had hoped this could be a long-term relationship. Her blinding anger got in the way; she was not able to deal with her disappointment because she did not recognize or acknowledge it. For many people, it is easier to feel angry than feel hurt and disappointed.

It also prevented Cheryl from hearing why Bill had to cancel, and this prevented her from resolving it satisfactorily. Anger generates a fight, flight, or freeze response. Cheryl chose flight in response to her anger. You cannot easily forgive if you are frozen or stuck in the avoidance or attack mode.

Often, a person's anger is conditioned by gender and cultural influences. In some cultures, men learn that it is okay to be angry, but not anything else. Some men are afraid they lose face if they show disappointment or sadness. For women, it's the opposite: it is better to talk about being disappointed than display anger. By not telling Bill why, Cheryl chose to hide her anger. It is not uncommon for women to repress overt expressions of anger. The fear is that society will view them as being bitchy rather than strong. As with all denials of personal truth, there is a price to pay.

What Is Seductive about Anger?

We use the word "seductive" deliberately. Anger is seductive because the feeling of power is addictive. Angry people feel more alive with the adrenaline rush associated with anger. Real personal power does not rely on anger, intimidation, or violence. Anger feeds your ego; it's all about you and how you feel, even though your focus appears to be on another person. Ironically, often your anger has little to do with the other person; your anger finds a target. Anger is seductive even though remaining in a constant state of anger is destructive.

Surprisingly, anger also seduces those who see it as harmful. Some people fear anger, so they keep it locked inside and nothing changes. They're doing nothing rather than acting honestly. They feel superior even though they harbour resentment. They want to look like a nice person. You can choose how to act on your anger in healthy ways that bring about forgiving and healthy reconciliation.

Two Sides of the Coin: Cathartic Anger, Toxic Anger

Anger can be volatile and confusing. You damage relationships and complicate forgiving when your anger is unfocused or out of control. However, if you don't address your anger and the issue that led to it, the end result is that you sabotage your ability to solve the problem. On the upside, releasing anger can be cathartic, giving you a sense of relief. This energy gives you the courage to state exactly what's on your mind. Sometimes anger serves as a way to free blocks in relationships.

Even though anger may feel cathartic, it can also seriously cloud your judgment, especially if it's linked to fear. When you're fearful, you'll likely blame and accuse others. Later, after an outburst, people say, "I wasn't thinking," as they know they acted rashly.

Sometimes people confuse tension or anger with feeling alive. The habitually angry person feels powerful in part because of the intensity of the emotion. But habitually angry people reinforce their anger by behaving in ways that tend to drive others away. Sometimes they don't realize that is what they're doing. Angry, prickly people are frequently in conflict, as they look for perceived injustices that become the norm as entrenched expectations. Sometimes it helps to ask, "How's this working for you?" The question works on two levels. First, it redirects the focus back to them rather than blaming others. Second, the question is perceived as non-threatening to their own authority. Sometimes it also helps deflate the energy around the issue so they see that anger and tension do not mean being alive.

Free-Floating Anger

Just as those with free-floating anxiety don't know the source of their anxiety (i.e., Generalized Anxiety Disorder) – people with free-floating anger don't know why they're angry. Their world is unsafe or unfriendly. Their anger acts like a lens through which they see their world, so they're quick to react in angry, defensive ways. It's possible they were hurt so early in life that they don't remember what happened. They do, however, continue to feel the emotion that has become so internalized that it rules them. Their anger has become so entrenched that others think it's a personality trait. They say they have a chip on their shoulder or a low boiling point. Their anger becomes an obstacle to growth, and forgiveness is difficult if not impossible.

Anger on the Inside, Anger on the Outside

As we saw, emotions are neutral; anger is neither good nor bad (T/S 10). The ability to express anger in appropriate situations and ways is a necessary human response. There are times when expressed anger is healthy (see Righteous Anger later in this chapter). But there are significant differences between outer expressed anger as a behaviour, and anger experienced inside, as an emotion.

Whether anger is inside or outside, once you learn to recognize it and handle it, you're able to make a conscious choice whether to act on it. You are in control, not your anger. By recognizing your anger, you have access to techniques that help control it, such as taming the tiger, where you train your anger so that you let it out appropriately. By taming it, you don't spend all your energy keeping it caged, fearing it will break out.

By learning to recognize anger, you're less likely to repress it. This is a good thing, as repressed anger affects your behaviour, as we saw with Cheryl. It can lead to depression or an embedded bitterness where you have a permanent chip on your shoulder, which tends to poison your interactions.

Repressed anger is different from controlled anger. Even though the person with repressed anger may appear to be calm and in control, their efforts to repress it come with a cost. They might suffer physically, with conditions like hypertension or ulcers. Sometimes the stress and inner tension make them look prematurely old. Occasionally, despite all their efforts, they have an outburst of anger that seems to come from nowhere. This happens, for example, when alcohol reduces their inhibitions or when the stress became too great and they can no longer restrain themselves.

Passive-aggressive Anger

Passive-aggressive people do not respond directly to issues of conflict, or to the person who angered them. For example, someone who's passive-aggressive may forget an event that is important to the person they are angry with. In terms of forgiveness, it takes more time to sort through the issues. In a relationship, sometimes it looks like they lack the courage to speak up. This makes it difficult to address issues, as the person may not even be aware they're angry. It's also difficult when passive-aggressive people become angry as a result of being criticized: for example, by shutting themselves off. If they think they're going to lose an argument, they don't want to play the game.

Why Are You So Bitter?

When someone else's behaviour did not live up to your expectations, you may be angry. If they hurt you, you may respond by becoming fearful or bitter, which may lead to passive-aggressive behaviour. A passive-aggressive response is a subtle or less obvious type of revenge that complicates forgiving. You cannot forgive and move forward if you don't acknowledge, let alone address, your underlying anger. You confuse the situation because you send mixed messages, which confuses the other person. Working through these responses is a necessary part of the process of forgiveness.

Covert Aggression

We coined the term "covert aggression" for those who express their anger by bringing others into the conflict, without the person they are angry with being aware of it (behind their backs). It is covert because on the surface it looks like they're looking for help; in reality, their actions are hurtful. Here, too, this makes it more difficult to sort through forgiveness issues. Under the guise of making things better, they bring more people into the conflict, which makes it worse. You may have experienced covert-aggressive situations with friends or family where you feel uncomfortable but could not put your finger on what was really going on.

Let's look at an example: Stacey and her husband, Tom, had been arguing and fighting for weeks. Underneath, Stacey was extremely angry, but she didn't try and address this with Tom. They got to the point where they were civil to each other only when in the company of others. One night, Stacey and Tom got together for dinner with Tom's best friend, Mike, and his wife, Beth.

When they were alone, Stacey told Beth she was worried about Tom. She asked Beth if the arguing could be the cause of Tom's difficulty in the bedroom. She asked Beth to keep this to herself, telling her Tom would be mortified if others knew, especially Mike.

From the outside, it looked like Stacey wanted to help Tom. She didn't seek medical advice, nor did she try and talk to her husband about this issue. Her anger and act of covert aggression was her betrayal of their privacy as a couple and the humiliation Tom would experience. By involving Mike and Beth, Stacey retaliated, but not in an open, direct manner. This added to the forgiveness issues she and Tom needed to work through.

Are You Overreacting or Reacting to Something Else?

By paying attention to your anger, by not repressing it, and by not acting out inappropriately, you are able to discover the cause of your anger. This is healthy. If, however, you direct your anger inward, you lose touch with and even deny your feelings. When this happens, the danger is that you overreact to minor events. If you find yourself over-reacting, ask, "Why did this upset me?" You might be reminded of a hurtful event that has not been resolved, or fear that it will bring up repressed memories. Similarly, if you think someone else overreacts to what you see as a minor event, it is best not to jump to conclusions. It may be that the other person interpreted the event in an entirely different way. For example, if you don't know a person had been violently mugged, it may seem they are unduly frightened whenever strangers approach.

Pastor James' Story: "A Funeral Faux Pas"

Once, when I was a young pastor, I was officiating at a funeral. The granddaughter, who was going to do the first reading, approached me just before the service and asked where she should sit. Normally, at funerals and weddings, I ask readers to sit close to the front so I can signal them when it is time. I thought I was being helpful, telling her to "Sit wherever you like," especially as I thought she might want to sit with her fiancé rather than right at the front. Later, I found out she was very angry. I greatly offended her, as she interpreted my comment as being dismissive. I was left wondering, "How could I do better next time?"

Had I known at the time, I would have said I was sorry. I was sorry for the misunderstanding. My apology would have been more of a gesture of sympathy, or caring, or even just wanting to explain, rather than to admit I did something wrong. I still don't think I did anything wrong. While I am sorry she was hurt, I recognize she needs to take responsibility for her own perceptions.

Then Comes Understanding

In brief encounters with others you don't know well, it's impossible to know all the factors involved. Typically, at funerals and weddings, people are emotional; as a result, they're more likely to misinterpret events. Strong emotions also affect how people experience something, including a comment meant to be helpful. While Pastor James thought he was being considerate, the granddaughter experienced his actions as dismissive. Too often, people are unable or unwilling to see their contribution in painful occurrences. It's easier to blame someone else than consider your part in it. The hint that something else was going on is seen by the vehemence of the granddaughter's anger.

We all face a dilemma when the other person demands an apology and we truthfully feel we didn't do anything wrong. In such cases, you can *respect* (T/S 1) where the other person is at when you take the high road. Try to remember that we all see events differently; your lens may prevent you from seeing the implications of your actions. It's one thing if you think an apology would help the other person feel better; it's another if you wouldn't be acting authentically. If you have to respond right away, take an objective stance; ask reflective and open-ended questions, such as "Is that the only way to interpret what happened?" "What would you have preferred me to do?" These questions do not imply you did something wrong; rather, you're trying to understand the other person. Hopefully, their struggle to answer these questions gives them a chance to process what happened.

The Gifts of Anger: Healthy, Accessible Anger

We speak of gifts here because anger is necessary; it serves us in healthy ways. Anger helps you to understand how you've been hurt and to respond appropriately. This kind of healthy anger is accessible to the person who's angry and the person they're angry with, so they both know where they are at. Neither one has to guess what's going on; there's no hidden agenda. With anger, you're able to move your relationship forward, in truth, to the point of forgiveness. Healthy, accessible anger brings about discussion, which in turn helps bring about resolution to conflict.

With healthy, accessible anger you can also consciously and freely choose not to act out the anger (see "Anger on the Outside," above). Choosing not to express your anger doesn't mean repressing it, but exercising restraint. You respond, but in a controlled and focused way, so the anger is expressed respectfully and appropriately. When you respond without thinking, you're acting on destructive urges rather than choice. The ultimate in living in freedom is the ability to make conscious choices about your behaviour.

It takes energy and conviction to resist the urge to lash out, to respond in anger. Those with real power have the choice not to use it, even at the risk of appearing weak. When you're angry, what are your intentions? Is your angry response based on a desire for a healthy resolution of the situation, or is your anger in control?

Anger Maturity

In the best-case scenario, people mature as they age, including what we call "anger maturity." A person with anger maturity is in touch with their anger, yet is not ruled by it. They know when they are angry, have insights into the cause of their anger, and can rationally decide how to express their anger in a productive way. Those without anger maturity maintain an adolescent, self-focused anger. Their anger is not in control, so you see temper tantrums or bursts of rage. Those with immature anger have little regard for the consequences or for those who get hurt in the process.

Righteous Anger

As we saw above, appropriate anger is a healthy reaction to wrongdoing. It helps bring about necessary change to right a wrong. Righteous anger helps moves people out of their complacency when they witness any kind of injustice. Righteous anger gives them the courage to be truthful, to state exactly what's on their mind, and this serves as a way to free blocks in relationships.

Objective Anger and Restorative Anger

Mature anger is also objective anger that helps see the situation for what it is. Objective anger is focused on what happened (the hurtful event) rather than being caught up in personal or emotional levels.

With objectivity, people remain grounded so that the other person's thoughts and opinions do not become the focus of their response. They are better able to recognize situations when the other person made a genuine mistake.

Objective anger and restorative anger are closely linked. While objective anger tends to be more individual, restorative anger brings about constructive social change. Restorative anger makes it easier to look at alternative ways to prevent harmful situations happening again, and to bring about justice. For example, it took a number of individual mothers whose children had been killed by drunk drivers to join together to form Mothers Against Drunk Driving (MADD) in order to do all they could to prevent others from suffering due to drunk drivers. In terms of forgiving, when your anger is objective, it's easier to forgive and reconcile when you focus on what happened rather than solely on the individual. This objectivity also makes it easier, when reconciliation occurs, to put healthy boundaries in place.

8

Frozen: When You Can't or Won't Forgive

Forgiveness can be messy. It can be overwhelming, especially when you have to deal with something you would rather avoid, or that you don't feel prepared to handle. As we pointed out earlier, emotions such as anger, bitterness, pride, vulnerability, and guilt contribute to difficulty in forgiving. You prolong your suffering by avoiding your feelings and issues. It's déjà vu: you have the same problem all over again. When you repeat mistakes, it's likely you haven't dealt with the underlying issues. You might joke about how you keep encountering the same problem until you get the lesson.

Meanwhile, everyone involved continues to suffer. If you have a problem with different people, and you're the common denominator, you may be the problem. Potentially, you are also the solution.

How Revenge Poisons Your Life

When you have an overwhelming desire to punish, and anger drives you, nothing can be resolved. It's a self-perpetuating cycle whereby anger intensifies the need for vengeance and punishment, and the desire for revenge increases anger. Worse, the desire for revenge creates tunnel vision; the danger is that you act as judge and executioner. It is imperative to get input from others to help you understand the situation correctly. Others help you take into account mediating factors, especially when you're blinded by your need for revenge.

People who think revenge is satisfying or necessary are not interested in forgiving. They're limited to one response: striking back. They're totally focused on that sole outcome, regardless of the cost to themselves or others. This narrow, mechanical thinking, where they won't consider other options, is destructive. As we saw, a healthy adult is one who responds appropriately.

Revenge breeds revenge, leading to more and more violence, which is a growing evil. Ironically, those seeking revenge become locked in a relationship with the ones they despise. They're locked in never-ending anger, violence, and bitterness. One way to stop this cycle is through forgiveness.

Revenge brings complications. Taking immediate retaliation has significant pitfalls; the avenger may not have all the facts, which they later come to regret. What they do in their act of vengeance may be even more damaging than what caused it.

If every human being retaliated for every hurtful act, humankind would not survive. Every accident, each misunderstanding, would generate negative responses followed by more violence. The increasing complexity of human interaction leaves little room for simplistic or knee-jerk retaliations. The arms race demands that we make every effort to understand, to consider others' mistakes as mistakes, and to seek peaceful solutions wherever possible.

Most often, revenge does not limit violence; revenge ups the ante. Centuries ago, the Hebrew (Old) Testament recognized the dangers in endless cycles of escalating violence. The passage "an eye for an eye" (Exodus 21:23-27), though often misunderstood, focuses on limiting or restraining revenge, rather than getting revenge. The "eye for an eye" idea was originally a radical concept: radical in that it suggests restraint. Restraint by keeping actions in proportion to the original offense, rather than escalating violence in a never-ending cycle of revenge, was the original intent of this biblical teaching. As helpful as this is, "eye for eye" thinking has limitations: whenever "an eye for an eye" is mistakenly used as a justification for getting revenge, the danger is that this leaves everybody blinded. Its real wisdom comes with the understanding that justice is not carte blanche retaliation, but must be in proportion to the offense. In other words, at best, "an eye for an eye" provides a basis for justice, healing, and finally, forgiveness.

Fortunately, wiser counsel stresses that even though the impulse for revenge is still there, we don't have to act on it. Whether or not there's a psychobiological, social, or evolutionary tendency towards retaliation, we're not chained to these tendencies. You can choose to resist the inclination to retaliate. You can do what you can to stop the cycle of violence. You can show strength by learning how to forgive and choosing not to retaliate.

Choosing Not to Take Revenge

Over the centuries, leaders in spirituality, religion, and philosophy have also looked at the idea of revenge. One idea they look at is that the desire for revenge is based in the belief that people *must* be punished for bad behaviour. Many teachers of wisdom warned of the dangers inherent in seeking revenge. Confucius wrote, "Before you embark on a journey of revenge, dig two graves."

Contemporary research on violence in the media suggests that people's comfort levels around violent and aggressive acts are increasing. Violent electronic games are commonplace. On one hand, the perception that society is increasingly unsafe and violent leads people to be more fearful and even become paranoid. On another level, this perception fosters a willingness to take vengeful actions in response to any and all aggressive acts. Road rage is just one example. On yet another level, people are increasingly attracted to the intensity of feeling that revenge elicits. The danger is that revenge is an adrenaline-driven activity and can be addictive for those caught in it.

Mark's Story: "Email Attack"

Mark had not received a single negative evaluation the entire 11 years he worked at the company. In fact, some of his work had been acknowledged publicly. Mark was completely taken aback as he read the email from his new boss, Murray. Mark was shocked to learn that, according to Murray, Mark had failed to provide necessary leadership for his position and had failed to fulfill the goals of the company.

To make things worse, his boss made it clear there was no possibility for further discussion. Mark was amazed to hear his boss mention he considered getting legal advice to have Mark fired. Murray made it clear he was not interested, even in an email, in what Mark had to say. Mark was left with damning allegations about his performance. He felt he had been judged and hung out to dry with no way to respond. As a result, Mark experienced tremendous self-doubt. He did not know what to think or what to do.

The content of the email and the refusal of his boss to meet with him brought Mark to counselling. He felt angry, confused, and depressed all at the same time. Mark was angry at the cold, impersonal way his boss communicated with him, and became increasingly angry when his attempts to speak to Murray were ignored.

Mark recognized that part of him wanted to lash out or get even. He did not plan on quitting quietly. He imagined walking into Murray's office unannounced, handing him his resignation, and letting Murray know what he thought of him in no uncertain terms. Mark struggled with the temptation to badmouth Murray to his colleagues, even though he thought this would be unprofessional. Even so, he was tempted to get back at Murray this way.

At the same time, Mark wondered where all that would leave him and the people who depended on him. He recognized his right to be angry at the completely unprofessional manner in which he had been treated. He was able to consider his options to resolve the situation. First, by looking at and talking about his anger, he did not repress or deny it. He decided to make a formal request to meet face to face with Murray. Mark refused to be treated as a non-person; he refused to be treated without dignity. Mark insisted on an opportunity to meet his accuser. Mark raised the bar at work with his demand to be treated in a respectful, professional manner.

Even after meeting with Murray, Mark learned he had more work to do to develop a reasonable working relationship with Murray. He knew it would be possible to work with this boss only if he remained in touch with, and made constructive use of, his anger rather than suppress his emotion. He did not back down, but neither did he over-react. Mark was pleased he had not quit in a fit of rage. He was glad he had not gone directly to the company president demanding that the president become involved.

As he acted in a controlled and focused manner, he was able to take appropriate action, including the direct request for a meeting. Even if the boss ultimately would not change his thinking about him, Mark knew where he stood. This meeting was a positive action resulting from his initial anger. If Mark had acceded to the refusal to discuss the criticism, this passive response to being attacked might have caused Mark to repress his anger, building on self-doubt. Even if the working relationship doesn't improve as a result of Mark's actions, it is less likely Mark will become depressed or bitter. Mark was able to assess his options with clarity, giving him a sense of power in his own career and life.

The Self-limiting Power of Negative Thinking

People don't always realize the extent to which they've been raised to think and act in predictable ways, according to certain expectations. Some expectations make forgiving difficult: It is not possible to forgive. It's not okay to forgive. It's all the more difficult if these expectations are based in cultural or societal assumptions. A warning sign that expectations get in the way is, for example, the hatred or distrust of a group of people, or members of a different religion. This is typical of "us and them" thinking, where anyone other than the group you belong to is the "other." The other is dehumanized to the point that forgiveness is not even considered.

Worse, it becomes easy to take pre-emptive revenge, where you hurt them before they can hurt you, because they're from the other group. News reports and history give us too many examples of the power of destructive thinking and pressure to hate others. We damage ourselves when we are stuck in or locked into negative, life-denying ways of thinking.

Resistance to Change

It's easy to remain stuck if you overlook the fact that change is almost always met with resistance. Generally, we take the path of least resistance. Sometimes it seems easier not to be responsible and do the hard work it takes to forgive and move on.

Generally, resistance is seen as an obstacle to healing. Resistance is a phenomenon well known to therapists. Resistant clients disagree or don't follow through with agreed upon treatment plans. They show up late or miss appointments altogether. Therapists overcome resistance in some cases by directly challenging the client, or by building in resistance as part of the treatment plan. More recently, some therapists are viewing resistance as a healthy response that protects the person from too much sudden change. New situations can be frightening to the client, even though a change may be healthier. Eventually, the client gives up failed problem-solving strategies and begins to trust the therapist's unfamiliar strategy.

If you automatically resist the tools and strategies for your forgiveness work, they may not be right for you at this time. Even if the tools don't make immediate sense to you, or they require you to take new actions, this does not mean they won't help. We are not going to suggest something you've already tried. It's more helpful to be prepared to think outside the box when you are stuck.

When You Are Hurt: The Difference between Acceptance and Doing Nothing

The healthy, functional adult operates on his or her own values and beliefs. This is the ideal; this is what we strive for. You give up personal power when you base your behaviour on another person's values. You've become reactive rather than proactive in your life.

Even though acceptance and doing nothing look similar, they are different responses to being hurt. When you do nothing because of outside pressure, you haven't forgiven; you've given up. If you think you will lose, so you do nothing, your response is based in fear.

For others, doing nothing is less about fear than ignoring the issue. It's possible that you do not respond to being hurt because you do not think the situation is worth it, or you ignore what happened because you've shut down emotionally. But there are psychological costs to doing nothing. When issues are repressed or don't get resolved, your self-esteem and ability to deal with problems takes a beating. This is quite different from the person who actively chooses to let it go when someone hurts them. Their actions are based in strength, not fear.

Hardness of Heart

One way to help understand hardness of heart is to see it as the unwillingness or inability to accept human weakness. Forgiving becomes all the more difficult if weakness is intolerable. Hard-hearted people are unforgiving. They believe they have the right to punish; indeed, they feel they must punish others for their own good. Hard-heartedness is judgmental and one-dimensional. Hardness of heart makes the person rigid, with no room for compassion, understanding, or the consideration of other options.

Self-image

Nobody likes to lose face. That is why it can be difficult to forgive, especially if you think forgiveness makes you look weak. It can be even more difficult to ask for forgiveness, especially if it feels humiliating. Each one of us protects our persona (our image) and our ego (our sense of self) at almost any cost. Many people avoid work on forgiveness because it affects both persona and ego.

It takes humility to apologize. Humility is not generally our first stance. It can also take humility to accept an apology, particularly in a narcissistic culture where image is imperative. The danger here is that you protect your image at all costs, even if you want to apologize (or accept an apology). When this happens, your self-image becomes toxic due to the fear or anger related to forgiveness. Both these emotions are destructively self-limiting.

Self-protection

Initially, not being able to forgive may be a form of self-protection. When you break your hand, you immobilize it to reduce pain and bring about healing. In a similar way, you sometimes immobilize emotionally around a particular hurt. Just as you would not leave a cast on your hand indefinitely, you need to remove the cast encasing your feelings to prevent your emotional life from withering. The overwhelming need for self-protection indicates outside help will be beneficial.

Obstacles to Forgiving Based on Bad Experiences

There are times when you have to face difficult personal obstacles before you can forgive. Some of these obstacles result from the combination of your personality traits and bad experiences. They prevent you from living the way you want; addressing them takes time, energy, and commitment. When you face setbacks, it doesn't feel like progress; it might feel like things are getting worse, not better. There are times when the best way to face these is to seek the help of a counsellor or therapist.

Learned Helplessness

You've probably met someone who's given up. They think nothing can be done, so they stop looking for a solution and stop trying. American psychologist, educator, and author Martin Seligman used the term "learned helplessness" to describe those who see no solution to their problems. The tragedy is when the situation changes and a solution becomes possible; the person is already convinced there is no point trying and therefore does not see the solution. Unfortunately, when learned helplessness becomes entrenched, it is associated with depression as well as other health-related issues.

Those who have tried to forgive but seem to be stuck may give up seeing any value in continuing to try. They learn to suppress their feelings. They also avoid any socializing that might be painful. They become bitter or sarcastic, isolating themselves in their pain. They inadvertently prevent healthy relationships from developing. When people say, "What's the use?" or "What difference will it make?" they have already given up.

Embodied Memories

Science continues to provide evidence of how the body and mind are one. We more readily accept that our bodies are not separate from our thoughts and feelings (see Chapter 6). The language we use shows how we have understood a body-mind unity on an intuitive level; we may say: he's a pain in the neck, she's a thorn in my side, what she did makes me sick to my stomach, he leaves me cold, and so on.

Even if you think you have moved on and are over whatever happened, your body may "think" differently. When we are no longer aware on a conscious level, the hurtful events have become embodied. In this case, you must address the hurt in other areas than just your mind. Thankfully, today there is greater recognition of how painful memories can cause significant stress, even illness. Anger, fear, and stress manifest as lack of sleep, over- or undereating, or developing ulcers, to name just a few. These hurts can also become manifest as headaches, autoimmune diseases, and other physical ailments.

You may not be aware you're holding on in this way. You may find yourself triggered by a sound, a scent, or something you see that is associated with the painful memory years later. You may recognize your tendency to overreact to certain triggers. Patti-Anne shared this experience: Years after I saw my townhouse burn to the ground, I could not tolerate the smell of smoke – it made me nauseous. You may not even remember the reason why you dislike something, such as a particular song or sound.

Many techniques are available to help deal with embodied pain. (See T/S 12.) You may begin a healthy exercise program, practise yoga, or find a meditation group for relaxation. You may seek out professional care with a physiotherapist or a registered massage therapist. You may explore other therapies, such as acupuncture, or address dietary options. Many people find work such as gardening or hiking to be as therapeutic as it is enjoyable.

Self-Efficacy

Forgiving is a necessary first step for your well-being and healing. When you believe in yourself, this promotes your self-efficacy. This is the opposite of learned helplessness, which prevents people from even trying to forgive. Noted psychologist Albert Bandura showed how an individual's beliefs are a significant factor when it comes to whether they will attempt a task. One way to increase your self-efficacy and build your confidence is by learning to use the Tools and Strategies in this book to bring about the changes you want in your life.

Evaluating Your Progress

Taking a long time to forgive doesn't mean you're doing something wrong. Various factors impact how long the process will take: how deeply you were hurt, the range of emotions involved, and past experiences. It can take longer if you need to work through cultural, societal, and religious expectations about forgiving. If you need to address issues with the person who hurt you, this takes time: What is their availability? Are they willing to talk? Are they able? Are they remorseful? Remember, forgiveness requires a willingness to embrace risk. All this takes time.

T/S 13: KNOW WHEN TO SEEK PROFESSIONAL HELP

Forgiving can take a lot of time and energy, or it can be short and sweet. Sometimes all it takes is someone saying, "I'm sorry," and it's done; you feel good and the relationship is repaired. However, sometimes the other person says they're sorry but the conflict and tension remain. Resolving the conflict may be beyond your abilities. You just may not have had the tools to bring about effective forgiveness and reconciliation. ➤

Most people resist addressing the painful areas of their life because these hold the memory of the original wound. If, over time, this wound is allowed to fester, it does more and more damage, which then affects other areas of their life. For example, this happens where abuse experienced as a child impacts an adult's ability to be in relationship with their partner. This kind of lingering effect is also evident in addictions. It's no coincidence that addictions counselling explores a person's past. The term "dry drunk" describes the person who, even though they are no longer abusing alcohol, hasn't dealt with his or her issues.

If you find that re-experiencing the trauma is just too much, or it seems pointless, then what? Are you tired enough to let go of your pain? The danger is becoming so drained by pain that you have no energy. You are immobilized, and over time, it is as if you are locked in. In this case you will benefit from outside help.

Some wounds are so deep that professional help is needed. Knowing this is available may be key to your health. Therapy involves change and confronting painful issues. This can be frightening, as you don't always know where the change leads. Still, you're free to make choices at the pace you are comfortable with. You may be able to hear something from a therapist or other professional that you can't hear from your spouse, family, or friends. If you feel stuck, and you are in touch with the complexities arising from being hurt, this is a healthy insight. It is far better to seek help than refuse therapy when you know it would help.

How to Benefit from Therapy

Finding the right therapist is not always easy. Do some research: ask your physician, your pastor or faith leader, or use the Internet. Professional associations for psychologists, social workers, and marriage and family therapists often provide referral services on their websites. If you're comfortable, ask friends if they can recommend a therapist.

If you're struggling with an issue related to forgiveness, ask the therapist how they understand these kinds of issues. If you feel uncomfortable with their response, explore those feelings with the therapist. If you continue to be uncomfortable, this may be a sign that this therapist is not right for you. On the other hand, the fact that you are resisting the changes that you fear therapy will challenge you to make could be a sign that the therapist is exactly what you need.

Before you enter therapy, consider what changes you want to make. When I was starting out as a therapist, an angry client once told me, "You're supposed to make me feel better, not worse!" Unfortunately, I missed an opportunity to talk about her expectations about therapy. We didn't discuss that she might feel uncomfortable before she felt better, which is a normal part of the process.

9

Handling Hurtful and Toxic Relationships

Power Imbalances in Relationships

When you're able to see a problem in a relationship and talk about it, you are on your way to a solution. It can be difficult to acknowledge that individuals in relationships are not always equal. It's easy to see when a relational imbalance of power is necessary: for example, parent–child, supervisor–employee, and student–professor relationships. These differences in power don't usually present a problem unless the boundaries become unclear.

Each relationship has its own set of boundaries, even though some boundaries are shared and others are distinct. Some boundaries are expressly set out, while others are more subtle. You see the power differences in relationships in terms of touch, for example. Touch serves as a barometer of power, as it can indicate support, rapport, or domination. If, for example, a boss touches an employee, all kinds of questions arise. Where the individual is touched indicates the type of relationship and what is being communicated. It is one thing to be patted by your spouse; it is entirely different to have a colleague touch you in the same way. Touch implies either control or a certain level of familiarity.

The power differential in relationships manifests itself in many ways. It shows up where one person needs the relationship much more than the other. This can be a primary need, such as a spouse needing to stay in a marriage to provide food and shelter for children. It can be an emotional need where a man or woman stays in an unsatisfactory relationship because he or she cannot bear the idea of being alone. Even in friendships, one friend may be more dependent on the other for socializing, and therefore has more to lose if the relationship ends; the dependent friend is reluctant to speak up when they are treated unfairly.

Generally speaking, the one who has the least investment in the relationship has the most power. Even though they are not always aware of it, the person who has the upper hand has a unique responsibility in the forgiveness process. When you hurt someone, you have upset the balance of power in the relationship. The wounded person feels embarrassed, perhaps even humiliated, and may be powerless to communicate this to the other person. Those with the most power should not assume all is well, as the least powerful person may not be able to speak honestly, let alone confront the other person about the issue.

When people are hurt, they often feel the need to get even; they instinctively feel they are in a less powerful position in the relationship. They may also feel that the other person owes them. The re-establishment of the balance of power in a relationship may not have occurred when forgiveness was first raised. Until you feel you are back on an equal plane with the other person, forgiving is difficult.

Addressing the relational power balance can be done in a number of ways. For example, when the offending person in the relationship acknowledges that they hurt the other person and asks what they can do to restore the relationship, this helps restore power to the other person.

"Poor me" syndrome, where there is a sense of power, comes from feeling like the wronged party. People most often feel sympathetic to victims. This leads to a different kind of imbalance of power where the victim becomes stronger. Some victims don't want to give up this kind of power, and they don't want to forgive and achieve a real reconciliation (Chapter 3).

Keeping Track in Relationships

When inequality exists in a relationship, it must be considered as part of the forgiveness process. The person with the least investment in the relationship has the least to lose if the relationship ends; therefore, the least invested person has subtler power. Psychologists use the ledger theory to describe how people evaluate their relationships with a mental ledger. Think of the way accountants keep track of what is owed and what is due. Having a sort of mental ledger helps you compare what you put into a relationship with what you get out of it. Most people want to keep their relationships in balance. They feel better not owing someone else and having no one owe them.

Each of us tries to balance our relationships in our own ways. When you feel the need to return a compliment immediately after receiving one, you are likely trying to re-establish the equilibrium in the relationship ledger. At times, you may want to distance yourself from a needy friend or an overly giving friend. Both needy people and overly generous people upset the balance. However, if you need to be needed, you will be attracted to needy people. If you have a lot of needy friends, you probably need them as much as they need you.

When You're Caught in the Middle

Having an outside vantage point is one of the easiest ways to see power imbalances in relationships. Have you ever felt uncomfortable when two friends asked you to take sides in an argument? Even though no one likes being in this position, most of us have sought support from a third party when we've been hurt. We hope they will sympathize with us or offer helpful advice. We feel better thinking we've dealt with the hurt. But triangulating – involving a third party to help us deal with anger or stress – is misleading if we don't deal directly with the person who hurt us.

In family therapy, the term "triangulation" describes a way to manage anxiety in a relationship. Family therapist Murray Bowen connected the ideas of triangle and strangulation. That third element can be another person: a spouse, a friend, or your therapist. It can also be a thing; your job or a cause you support. This allows you to manage anxiety without handling the troubling situation. Your energy is directed to someone, or something else, rather than the person who is the source of the stress.

Unless the third person de-triangulates out of the situation, the person suffering the stress remains stuck. This is why good therapists stay neutral, which allows their clients to go back to the real source of their anxiety. A therapist's focus is not solely to make their clients feel good; rather, the therapist challenges clients to deal constructively with the real issues.

In terms of forgiveness, triangulation confuses the issue and becomes an additional forgiveness issue. Triangulation makes forgiveness feel like trying to nail Jell-O to the wall; it's all talk around the issue with people other than the one who hurt you, and still nothing is done about the real issue. When actions are taken to de-triangulate, the movement towards forgiveness shifts in a positive direction: the focus is on the person who hurt you, rather than others. You are then able to deal with the anxiety and stress. When you take responsibility for your part, this helps bring resolution.

Aggressive Triangulation

To help you see possible challenges for forgiving and reconciliation, we would like to introduce the concept of aggressive triangulation. Here, a third person is openly used as a weapon to hurt the other person in their presence. You sometimes see aggressive triangulation in couples. Let's look, for example, at Jim and Betty. Jim constantly denigrates his wife in front of other people. Those who have to hear him criticize her don't want to do or say anything to add to Betty's embarrassment.

Here's the problem: if you remain silent, you are colluding with Jim's aggressive triangulation, like it or not. As the third party, you're angry because you feel forced to be silent out of politeness, or not wanting to make it worse.

There are ways to de-triangulate in such a situation; you could say, "I don't appreciate this. You guys need to try to get along, at least in my presence." Being more direct, you can say, "If you continue to do that, I'm out of here." People who give honest responses even if it seems impolite or rude avoid these traps. If Jim says, "I was kidding," then you are put on the defensive, and Jim still doesn't get it. If Jim says,

"Well, maybe that was uncalled for," then he has de-triangulated with the person who called him out.

While they look similar, there are significant differences between covert aggression and triangulation. Triangulation is used to manage the tension in a relationship; even though it involves others, it's not necessarily intentionally subversive. A person who is covertly aggressive has a hidden agenda to do harm in the guise of help. A person who aggressively triangulates openly manipulates others to bring about harm. Covert aggression is similar to passive aggression in that the actions are not instantly recognizable as being aggressive.

Covert aggression damages another person in some significant way, such as their reputation or self-esteem. When another person is told information that is a personal part of another relationship, both the person who hears it and the person it is about are hurt. It likely puts the person who has been told in a bind: they can't tell, and they can't not tell. In this and other ways, covert aggression violates personal and relationship boundaries.

Reclaiming Me

When a relationship hits the breaking point, especially when you're angry, it is normal to withdraw the part of you that you had invested in the relationship in order to protect yourself. When you're not emotionally involved in the same way, you're not as vulnerable; the other person can no longer push your buttons. However, this pulling back is not focused on reconciliation.

In a healthy relationship, there's both give and take. When you end a relationship, you withdraw emotional involvement. When you reclaim yourself, this doesn't mean you become jaded or bitter. Reclaiming means you respect your experience, your truth, and the truth of the relationship. You've learned from the experience and moved on. By doing this, you are able to forgive yourself and the other person.

You may have heard divorced people say, "All men are rotten," or "There are no good women." Some people just can't get over a bad relationship. Their bad experience makes them self-protect to such an extent that they're afraid to try again. Even if they now have a relationship, they can't enjoy it, because part of them is emotionally unavailable. Working through forgiveness issues offers you an opportunity to free yourself from past hurts and to live life more fully.

Grief is part of being alive and an important aspect of the forgiveness process. What you might interpret as a difficulty with forgiving may be a normal and healthy grieving of a loss, rather than a problem with your ability to forgive. When you have been hurt, you must work through many kinds of loss: the loss of the relationship, the loss of friendship, and the loss of trust. Generally speaking, women tend to cry and seek comfort from a supportive friend; men tend to move into fix-it mode and become busier as a way of working through their grief. While there are general patterns when it comes to grieving, the way you grieve and how long you need to grieve is completely personal.

T/S 14: ADDRESS POWER IMBALANCES AND REGAIN YOUR SENSE OF SELF

When you've been hurt in a relationship, your relationship is not the same. The balance of power between you has shifted. As a result, you may feel withdrawn or fearful. If you don't recognize what's happened, your sense of self in the relationship becomes progressively worse. This may contribute to a sense of victimhood, where you become weaker or somehow less valuable in the relationship. As a way to address these issues, use the following as a checklist:

1. Admit the problem: Write in your own words what has changed between you. Ideally, if both sides admit from their respective points of view what has changed, it's easier to work things out. When things are clearer, you're able to make a positive shift in the relationship. ➤

2. Own your feelings: You must own how you feel as a result of being hurt. You may feel shame, anger, disappointment, and so on.

3. Listen: Listen to the other person's point of view, even when it's painful. This is necessary so you can work through your respective issues. If either of you is stuck in self-justification, it's harder to address the power imbalance and heal the relationship.

4. State your needs: In order to rebalance your relationship, state what actions you need from the other person. This might include their apology, followed by a conversation about what needs to be done. This includes what actions are needed to reassure you it won't happen again, how to make amends, or agreeing to seek counselling.

Reconciliation

Reconciliation is more complicated when you've been hurt and the balance of power has changed. It adds to the confusion if you fight over trivial matters and avoid addressing more threatening issues. If you never talk about the real problem, this is where unresolved grief comes from. In order to fully reconcile, you need to grieve loss on many levels, including your previous expectations about the other person and about your hopes and dreams for the now damaged relationship. If you don't address these, even though you think you've forgiven each other, the underlying problems prevent a real reconciliation.

In any relationship, the willingness to reconnect is a choice. Until you are ready to do the work, you will be stuck in an incomplete, perhaps even a flawed reconciliation. The deeper the wound experienced in a relationship, the longer and more complex the process of healing and reconciliation will be.

Forgiving does not mean ignoring that actions have consequences. Sometimes you have to maintain the relationship with the person who hurt you: for example, at work. However, the relationship is different, in that you now have new information about the other person. Until you have an opportunity for the person to earn back your trust, you may forgive them, but the relationship needs to be rebuilt. In an extreme situation, such as with a chronic liar, you take that into consideration in future interactions even though you choose to forgive them. This is not punishment; you are being realistic about your own safety and well-being.

Power Imbalances in Other Relationships

Significant differences in power exist when you're in a relationship with someone who represents an institution, such as a church, school, university, corporation, or government. You will feel alone if you are hurt by this institution-person; they have the power and weight of the in-stitution behind them. You may hope the authorities will investigate the role of the person who hurt you and address your needs. In other words, you hope the wrong against you will be righted, and the institution-person will face appropriate consequences for the harm they caused. Sadly, at times there's a cover-up. The differences between the power of a group and that of an individual undermines and intimidates. This is devastating and may lead to different levels of forgiveness issues: with the person who hurt you, and with the institution that made it worse.

For Those Seeking Forgiveness

Begin by acknowledging that you hurt the other person. Be open to what they are experiencing and any related issues they may have. Acknowledging your role is not easy. It may challenge your belief, for example, that you seldom make mistakes. You must also acknowledge that you are responsible for your actions. Offering excuses such as "She (he) made me do it" doesn't help. Some people, even though they're sorry, can't say it. Doing so would be to admit a mistake, which is too difficult for them. The first step is to admit that you messed up; with-out that, you cannot enter into dialogue with the person you hurt. The problem is, it is seldom entirely 100% your fault. In most cases, the blame is shared. People hold onto the fact that it was not all their fault as a way of holding onto their old self-image.

When you seek forgiveness, you must address changes in the relationship. The person who was hurt may experience a loss of power, prestige, sense of value, or personal authority. When you seek forgiveness, the third task involves letting go as well as grieving that loss. You have to accept a more realistic perception of yourself and of your relationship.

The process of forgiveness requires grieving in two ways: the loss of both your shiny self-image and the shiny image of your relationship. Sometimes this means admitting to yourself that you have faults and the relationship had problems.

When Someone Wants Your Forgiveness

When someone seeks forgiveness from you, you also have tasks. First, you must acknowledge how you have been hurt. Second, you must grieve the loss of your original perception of the person: for example, as being "just too nice to do something like that." In many cases, particularly with couples, grieving the loss of your image of the other person is difficult. Sometimes you may think to yourself, "Never in a thousand years could I imagine him (her) doing that." You also have to acknowledge your own need for forgiveness, for we all make mistakes; in this way, you become more open to forgiving others.

Start by making a list of the people you have hurt, whether you hurt them on an emotional level or harmed them by your actions. Be sure to also include those times when it was your inaction, when you failed to do something, that hurt or caused harm. This is inspired, in part, by our work helping others as they work through the eighth step in Alcoholics Anonymous (AA).

The purpose of the list is not to make you experience guilt or shame, nor is this exercise designed to justify the other person's actions. Making the list helps remind you where you have hurt others and allows you to get in touch with the fact that we all make mistakes. This helps you forgive others.

After creating the list, ask yourself what caused you to act (or not act) in a way that hurt someone. Did you intend to do harm? Did you forget the other person's need? Did you not realize your behaviour would hurt others? Do themes emerge from reflecting on these experiences? Being aware of your ability to hurt others can lead to healing when you are trying to forgive.

You, too, must address the power imbalance that has taken place between you. For example, when someone lets you down, they say they owe you. They don't mean they owe you money – they wish to make up for their actions. They recognize that you have been hurt.

Forgiveness of Self

Forgiveness of self is the cornerstone: if you can't forgive yourself, you can't forgive other people. On a superficial level, forgiving yourself seems easy, but it's not. It involves humility, personal awareness, acceptance of self, and the courage to confront the truth. The willingness to address issues is an opportunity for personal growth.

If you're intolerant of personal weakness or personal limitations, you will not easily forgive yourself. Part of forgiving yourself requires humility: you need to acknowledge and accept that you made a mistake or did something wrong. When your self-image doesn't leave room for error, this makes it very difficult to forgive yourself. The ability to be self-critical depends on your self-concept. To forgive yourself, you have to accept what you've done and accept that you're not as good, integrated, mature, or savvy as you'd like to believe.

You also need compassion. Sometimes, in an effort to deal with your faults, you may continue to self-sabotage and punish yourself. How much punishment do you have to endure before you can forgive yourself and let go? Punishing yourself is similar to taking revenge, but in this case you are the accused, the judge, and the executioner.

Many people live with deep regret and struggle to forgive themselves for what they did when they were young. While you can't relive the past, you can find new ways to understand it. Judging your past actions in light of the present is unfair. You made the decision or acted based on who you were at the time. You are being overly harsh when you judge past mistakes without recognizing that you now have a new understanding.

Part of the experience of growing older is seeing young people make the same kinds of mistakes you made. Compassion for others becomes easier, because you've been through similar situations. Each time you are understanding and compassionate to a person who hurt you, you are also forgiving yourself.

Forgiving yourself when the person you hurt in the past refuses to forgive you presents special challenges. You must always recognize the right of the other person not to forgive you. You may have to grieve the loss of this relationship.

If you have done everything in your power to apologize, make amends, and make restitution for damages, then you're in a position to begin to forgive yourself. Those who try to forgive themselves as part of a program such as AA often undertake some form of restitution to the ones they've hurt. For the sake of your mental health, work on learning from your mistakes and forgiving yourself so that you can live constructively. Self-forgiveness, like all forgiveness, does not involve forgetting. You remember what you've done and continue to take responsibility for it. Religious people who address forgiveness of self also seek forgiveness from God as part of their forgiving process.

Handling Shame and Guilt

When you act in ways that you know are wrong, you feel guilty. In an effort to deal with the resulting guilt and stress, you may minimize either the seriousness of your actions or the event itself. You may tend to avoid the issue by rationalizing or intellectualizing, saying things like "What I did is just a part of being human." These kinds of behaviours are defence mechanisms. By doing this, you avoid an opportunity for personal growth.

If you feel guilt or shame, one of the worst things to do is keep the feelings to yourself. This is true whether it's about what you did or what was done to you. As hard as it is, share what you feel guilty or shameful about with someone you trust. You will not be able to forgive if you believe what happened is shameful or if you believe what happened would dishonour your family or betray your religious, philosophical, or cultural beliefs.

If you feel shame or guilt, resist the temptation to judge yourself too quickly. Instead, reflect on what you've learned. When you ask yourself what caused you to act the way you did, you will begin to see mistakes as opportunities to learn rather than as entrenched failures. At some point, did you pass the point of no return in your behaviour? Looking at this will help you see how to prevent similar mistakes in the future.

Bringing Self-forgiveness to Life

At first glance, self-forgiveness might seem self-indulgent. Far from it! As part of self-forgiveness, decide if you need to make a meaningful gesture or do something as your way of righting a wrong you've done. This is in addition to seeking forgiveness from the person or persons you hurt.

There are no set rules for self-forgiveness. What works for one person may not work for another. Your gesture must relate to the event and feel authentic. For example, Gandhi once answered a Hindu man who was overcome with grief and guilt because he had killed a Muslim child during a religious uprising. The man asked Gandhi what he could do. Gandhi advised him to take a Muslim orphan and raise him as his own child. Gandhi added that he must raise the child in the Muslim faith. Gandhi helped the man do what he could to redeem his horrific act.

Those who do the Twelve Step program of AA follow steps for reconciliation and for restitution for past behaviour. Many people, not just recovering alcoholics, have regrets about past behaviour. Some people may regret their actions towards parents, siblings, or colleagues. With greater maturity, they realize the error of their ways. They may understand they are evaluating past behaviour using today's values, but they still feel guilty. Without a ritual or a way to meaningfully demonstrate their desire to make reparations, their forgiveness process is impeded. Depending on the situation, a meaningful gesture and symbolic act could be making a donation to a charity that is important to the one who has been hurt, or getting involved in helping others. You cannot undo the past, but you can honour those you've hurt.

Forgiveness Issues in Workplace Relationships

The work-based relationship is somewhat of an anomaly. Friendships develop due to the many hours spent together, but often the relationship is situational rather than intentional. Sometimes a work relationship is arbitrary; without the common element of work, there would be no relationship. With some relationships there's a hidden agenda. Relationships with co-workers can be strained due to changes in rank and company politics. Other differences in relationship dynamics depend on whether you work with or for someone.

This is not to suggest that work-based friendships are not valuable or meaningful. Colleagues can become friends, but the two parties must have mutually acknowledged boundaries. In terms of forgiveness, the workplace adds to the complexity. Even though you may form social friendships at work, they're distinct from regular friendships. For example, at work you may be placed in a position where you have to compete with your friend (such as for promotion). One consideration is whether the friendship will survive conflict. No matter what happens, you can't walk away from the relationship at work. When conflict arises with a personal friend, you have more choices to resolve it (or not). When there are difficulties in the work relationship, you have to get along; you must work together, like it or not.

The challenge in terms of forgiving is when the workplace relationships become emotional and personal rather than professional. When the boundaries becomes blurred, it's hard to deal with personal comments that are shaming, such as "I expected more from you" rather than saying, "This project was not done to company standards."

Dealing with Conflict at Work

When you experience conflict at work, consider what happened and how it happened. Let's imagine that your boss criticizes you because you were late. Even though you might understand the criticism, you're offended by how they expressed it. Separating the what and the how is easier in the workplace than in a friendship. Take, for example, the issue of Bob being chronically late. Some of his friends wonder if Bob doesn't really care. Other friends recognize that Bob has time management problems, so it's not personal. However, Bob's being late at work is a different matter. His boss has to challenge him directly, in a way that friends would not. If, however, the boss humiliates Bob in front of his colleagues, it feels as if it is a personal attack. Here's another example. If you were laid off from a job because the company is downsizing, it's painful, but not personal. If you are laid off and treated without respect and humiliated in the process, it feels personal. In both cases, how you were laid off impacts how you feel. When the how part did not feel personal, it's easier to focus on the what, which is your job loss, and move forward in your life without bitterness.

Not all managers and supervisors are trained to be leaders. Their leadership style may compound the issue. For example, many managers are primarily task oriented; if you are relationship orientated, you will likely experience hurt until you understand the dynamics of work-based relationships.

If someone at work appears to be overreacting, other issues likely hook him or her. Recall how fear causes people to react in unexpected ways. People at work are afraid of many things: losing their edge, being demoted, or being made redundant. While fear does not excuse their behaviour, awareness helps you respond in a more professional way.

Communication Skills in the Workplace

Being able to work through difficulties and be forgiving – whether this involves forgiving your boss or your colleagues – is crucial if you are to develop satisfying work relationships. The Tools and Strategies in this book also help you to constructively handle conflict at work. Non-labelling language keeps you focused, especially at times when conflict seems personal and less professional.

Before you meet to resolve conflicts, take steps to help you understand the issue. Avoid using only email, as it tends to be cold and is easily misunderstood. When you meet, pay attention to factors besides the words, such as non-verbal communication. When you respond to questions, phrases like "Help me understand why you did what you did" or "It would help me if the following were addressed" are more likely to bring about resolution. Communicating in this way demonstrates your willingness to understand and your respect (T/S 1) for the other person. Using these phrases encourages you to process the issue and to bring meaningful closure to the conflict.

When workplace conflicts arise, stay focused on workplace or professional behaviour expectations. Keep your focus on what you would like to see changed to improve the workplace. Take responsibility for what you need to be done to solve the problem. If it's appropriate, name your feelings by saying, for example, "I feel frustrated if you don't turn your work in on time." This is more productive than saying, "You're disorganized."

All Relationships Are Not the Same

As we've seen, you benefit by not confusing the different kinds of relationships you have in the family, with friends, and at work. It is possible that you also have another kind of relationship: over the years, you develop a relationship with the company itself. How do you forgive a company when you've been hurt by its actions? For example, let's say the Acme Company fires all the workers in one of their plants. If you've spent your whole life working for Acme, even when they say being fired wasn't personal, it feels personal.

Perhaps you felt committed to a company only to discover it was not reciprocal. As we saw, it's not only what's done but how it happened that affects how you feel and how you view yourself. You may feel as betrayed by the company as when a person hurts you. This presents a special set of forgiveness issues to sort through. Begin by sorting out the issues as you see them.

Mistrust versus Lack of Trust

As emotions can run high with workplace issues, it's important to see differences between mistrust and a lack of trust and your expectations (see Chapter 2). While mistrust implies a malevolent intention, a lack of trust implies you simply don't know what to expect. A lack of trust occurs when you don't know the other person well enough to build a trusting relationship and you're understandably cautious. Mistrust occurs in established relationships where there are unresolved violations of trust.

Some of the related workforce forgiveness issues include being passed over for promotion, losing your job, forced retirement, or betrayal by a colleague. Feeling betrayed by a business associate is devastating. It could simply be that a colleague or supervisor takes credit for your work. In more serious cases, a supervisor seriously undermines the effectiveness of the employee to do their job by withholding important information.

Workplace Munchausen by Proxy

The colleague who deliberately sabotages your work so they look good is what we call Workplace Munchausen by proxy. We base this syndrome on Munchausen by proxy, a relatively rare condition where a parent physically harms their child so they can win the admiration of medical personnel who are treating the child.

Workplace Munchausen by proxy occurs when a supervisor deliberately sabotages an employee's work, forcing the employee to depend on them to solve the problem. In serious cases, the employee becomes dependent on the supervisor to get them out of trouble. This presents a double whammy for the person who wants to forgive not only the sabotage, but the betrayal by their supervisor. Let's look at John's experience.

John's Story: "Set up for Failure"

John was hired as a manager to oversee the student residences. John's boss, the Director of Student Services, was very helpful; John began to consider him a friend. Several months later, the director emailed John the name of a student and a request to find accommodation. John, in an effort to please his boss, gave the student preferential accommodation, moving the student to the head of the line, even though this was against the rules.

The director failed to mention that this student had been expelled from residence four years earlier. It wasn't long before the student created serious problems again, and John had to let him know he would be expelled for his behaviour. When John met with him, the student threatened to sue the university, claiming he was being discriminated against.

Because the student threatened legal action, John needed the director's assistance to deal with this problem. Ultimately, John was called to explain the situation to the university president. Even though there had been no discrimination, and the student had caused problems, the student won. It looked like John had mishandled the situation and the director saved it. The president praised the director, as he wanted at all costs to avoid a lawsuit.

John struggled to forgive his director as he had to work for him. John learned the hard way that the director could not be trusted. If the director had followed procedure and shared the student's file, John would never have given the student accommodation. John was bitter that the director never acknowledged that he withheld background information so it looked like he bailed John out. John was angry that the director wanted to be seen as the rescuer and gained the president's admiration.

10

Forgiveness and Victimhood

The Cost of Victimhood

In terms of forgiveness, when abuse occurs, both the nature of the abuse and the consequences must be addressed. If not, the one who was abused shuts down, locked into pain, anger, and lingering victimhood. Whether the abuse was emotional, spiritual, physical, or sexual, the consequences manifest on multiple levels, including emotional, psychological, spiritual, and physical ones.

Sometimes people who were abused become stuck in a self-incriminating mode. They take responsibility for events over which they had no control. They feel locked in and can't forgive because the abuser does nothing to seek forgiveness. Until the person who was abused understands that *they* benefit by forgiving, they remain locked. They also benefit from knowing that they can forgive for their own peace of mind, but this does not mean they have to forget what happened or reconcile with the abuser.

Victims with no interest in working through the issues pay a high price. Some handle the stress by becoming chronic callers to distress lines. Some become "yes, but" people; they want to talk about their problem but are not willing to make any effective efforts to resolve it.

Trying to help a "yes, but" person can be frustrating, as they ignore your suggestions. You can't help because they don't want help. They don't say no outright; they say, "Yes, but" your suggestion won't work for this or that reason. If you suggest that they seek help from a therapist, they say they can't right now. They have lots of reasons: they haven't got the money or the time. Eventually you realize that they want you to sympathize and to listen and that you're both wasting your time going over the same issue again and again.

The Blame Game: Don't Shoot the Messenger; Don't Blame the Victim

All too often, those who dare to tell the truth, to talk about abuse, are shunned by family members and the community, including their church, as troublemakers. For the abused, to be treated like this means being revictimized. Worse yet, as whistleblowers, they're accused of causing a problem. It takes courage to come forward about sexual abuse, especially if the accused is a popular priest, scout leader, respected teacher, or family member. More problems arise when other people blame and direct their anger at the whistleblower rather than investigate the allegation.

Blaming is doubly destructive when victims are blamed to protect other people's sense of safety. Those who blame think the victim caused their own misfortune, as if all it takes to be safe is to avoid doing what the victim did. This gives the blamers a false sense of security and makes them hypercritical of the victim. How many sexual assault victims have been blamed because they were wearing the wrong clothes, or were at the wrong place at the wrong time? This blame mentality revictimizes the victim.

Maria's Story: "I Know Who I Am"

Maria was a shy, soft-spoken woman who escaped from a war-ravaged country. The room went quiet when Maria spoke about what happened to a group of women who also escaped violent and brutalized countries. Maria talked about her experience when soldiers left her village after a rampage of mutilating, raping, and killing. She told of the village shame; she spoke of how some people said she was not wanted after being defiled.

She slowly looked around the room at each of the women, most of whom were looking down at the floor. Maria said, "I want you to know. Those soldiers hurt my body. They used my body. But I'm still me. The men who raped me harmed my body, but they hurt their own souls."

Maria's incredible sense of dignity did not depend on another person. She was free. By sharing her story with women who had suffered brutality as she had – both by being raped and in how others treated them afterwards – she helped them see they could heal. The tears flowed freely. Her sharing and saying out loud some of the women's deepest anguish gave others words for what had been unspeakable before.

Fascination with Victims

Victimhood is complex; it may seem strange that being a victim brings energy with it. Some people are drawn to victims in order to help them. For others, victims offer a darker attraction; the pain and suffering provide a rush. You see this when people come to gawk at accidents rather than help.

Unfortunately, victims are also entertainment. Over the years, too many TV shows focus on actual victims and their plight. The attraction of these shows centres on the revelation of some painful secret. To ensure an exciting show, opposing people are brought in, such as the other woman/man or estranged family members. In some shows, the crowd actively participates by booing or clapping after each individual tells their story.

The fascination – the seductive power of watching victims – derives, in part, from the adrenaline rush associated with extreme emotions. The seductive power for the victim comes from the attention they receive. Any kind of attention, whether it is affirming or critical, is better than nothing. The danger for the person who was hurt or abused is becoming a lifelong victim rather than a survivor.

The Power in Victim Status

Surprisingly, there is power in victim status. It's not always true that victims are poor, suffering, powerless individuals. Victim status provides an identity, not just for the victim but for those attracted to help them, and brings with it unspoken expectations. Most people are more gentle and generous with victims; they don't want to cause more pain. They don't want to do anything to further victimize the person. As understandable as this is, this expectation can be very seductive; the danger is that the person may use their victim status to get their own way. They feel entitled; something is owed to them. Often, they are not conscious of this; to confront them directly will likely result in denial. Even acknowledging the victim's power in this way is seen as politically incorrect, disrespectful, or insensitive. By finding the courage to look at their identifying as a victim, they are able to remove blocks. When they have the courage to do so, they begin their healing.

Crowned Victims

Some people revel in their victim status. They get hooked on their identity as a martyr because it empowers them. Knowingly or not, they manipulate others through guilt. Sometimes it takes another victim to challenge them to move on, to heal. There is nothing better than a recovering alcoholic to help another alcoholic move beyond "stinking thinking." There is nothing like an addict to confront another addict in dysfunctional beliefs and strategies.

Crowned victims have been hurt and don't want to do anything to make things better. The crown in effect says, "Look how much I've suffered." The danger is that they get stuck there. Crowned victims blur personal boundaries because they feel compelled to share their woes with everyone they meet. They need sympathy to such an extent, they come to demand it. As a result, they limit themselves: "I can't do any better; I've been badly treated." They expect you to listen to their problems and support them in this thinking.

For victims, it makes absolute sense to provide support following trauma and as they move towards healing. However, the crowned victim becomes an expert in being a victim. They resist healing. They fear change; they don't know what they have to give up as part of their wounded identity. Sadly, this crown keeps them from a healthier life.

Festering Victims

You can tell a festering victim by the chip on their shoulder. Their anger is always just below the surface. They consistently interpret other people's actions in a negative way. This festering affects everyone: for example, the angry parent takes it out on their children. They think they have the right to hurt others because they themselves have been hurt. This kind of victimhood can also be handed down, such as when family members hold grudges because of some wrong inflicted generations ago. Tragically, for festering victims, a family member who has worked towards forgiveness or resolving the issue is viewed as a betrayer.

Dominating Victims and Passive-Aggressive Victims

Dominating victims direct their anger outwards. They lash out or actively go out to hurt others. Like the festering victim, the dominating victim carries a chip on their shoulder. Passive-aggressive victims are not as easy to recognize. Their aggressive victim behaviour is subtle. It isn't always apparent how they go about getting their way, as their anger is expressed indirectly or by cold silence. They thwart honest communication, which might help them move beyond victimhood.

If You Struggle When Someone Else Cries in Any Kind of Conflict

If you struggle when others cry in your presence, ask yourself, "Why are they crying? What does the person who is crying expect me to do: provide sympathy, solve a problem, or just listen?" This helps direct your response. It helps overcome feelings of manipulation or powerlessness that can impact forgiving.

Perpetual Revictimizing

When a person staunchly remains a victim, this meets many needs. As victims, others have to go easy with them, afraid of hurting them or of adding to their pain. This puts victims in a position of unassailable power. While it may seem like power, it is actually self-imposed isolation: nobody else can be honest with them for fear that the victim can't bounce back. There are no-go zones in conversation, which limits the integrity of relationships. It also limits other people, because they can't speak their truth, either. In this way, people around the victim become submissive. The victim has in effect limited all their relationships, not just the one involved in the original circumstance. This is how victims continue to revictimize themselves.

Self-victimization

Some people self-victimize by not wanting to be seen as quitters. As a result, they stay in unhealthy environments and even dangerous situations, even when leaving is the best decision. They do not recognize dead ends. They have gone as far as they can with the job or relationship. It is time to move on and allow someone else with different skills and experiences to become involved. To continue a project or an unhealthy relationship when your health suffers is self-destructive. Leaving can be a courageous, pro-active move.

Tragically, some people who have been victimized will revictimize themselves over and over again. A particular danger for those who are depressed is when they think and fantasize about suicide. Psychologists call this "suicidal ideation." A person with suicidal ideation has internalized the wound to the point that they are unable to pinpoint how they were hurt. This kind of distorted thinking requires professional intervention. This type of internalized core victimization is self-destructive on all levels; body, mind, and spirit.

Moving from Victim to Survivor

It is a different situation for people who have worked through painful events where there has been some sort of resolution and healing has occurred. Whatever happened to them no longer dominates their lives. The painful event has become a part of their life rather than defining it. Survivors think about the event in an informed way rather than being controlled by it. They are able to respond to events rather than simply react. Moving from victim to survivor brings a sense of freedom, of choice.

11

Forgiveness after Divorce, and All That Follows

orgiveness for those in a committed relationship can be one of the more intimate acts either party will experience, because in this context, forgiving is love in action. For couples who have strong feelings about entering into a fully committed relationship, it makes a difference knowing both of them will do all they can to make it work. This level of commitment and shared ground rules makes it is easier to forgive as they share the same assumption that the other person is doing all that they can to maintain the relationship (see Chapter 2). However, forgiving in a committed relationship is all the more painful when a couple divorce.

The Divorce Minefield

When it comes to forgiveness, divorce is a minefield. In the aftermath, not many areas in your life remain untouched. Splitting up is no less painful for those in common-law marriages or long-standing relationships. For simplicity, we refer to the challenges after breaking up as "divorce." Divorce tends to bring out the best and worst in people, sometimes at the same time. Whenever a relationship or a marriage ends, both the personal and the social aspects of life have the potential to blow up.

At the personal level, divorce impacts your sense of self. Divorce hits at who you were as wife or husband, as well as your desirability. It also challenges your role as a parent. The breakdown and split impact your extended family and can impact your life at work and your faith life. When a divorce occurs, your social life is also affected. No matter how careful you are, divorce intensifies forgiveness issues. Divorced people who know about these pitfalls can chart their course of action to more effectively deal with them.

T/S 15: MONITOR YOUR EXPERIENCE IN STRESSFUL SITUATIONS

If you're going through a divorce or another traumatic situation, keeping a journal of your thoughts and feelings helps you focus and sort through the issues. Even if it seems difficult, write about what happens as the situation unfolds; this serves as a release, and it helps you sort through conflicting emotions. Remember; you do this to monitor and get in touch with your feelings, not as a way to remember all the things your ex has done wrong.

For those whose divorce is long past, write your story about your experience. Follow the same guidelines as in T/S 2. Here, too, writing your story is therapeutic; it provides you with another perspective and options you had not considered before. It helps you get in touch with feelings you've repressed and see emotional traps. This helps avoid missing some of the forgiveness issues that are blocking you.

Keep in mind that even though writing can be difficult if painful feelings are awakened, this is where the healing begins. If you feel alone, look for support groups that focus on healing rather than people who remain stuck in anger about their situation. While it's helpful to have a place to vent, it is not helpful to remain at that stage for an extended period.

Handling Your Feelings after Divorce

For some people, divorce brings about suffering in ways they never anticipated. The divorce proceedings make things even worse, as it's embarrassing when personal information is made public or twisted out of context. It's highly probable that you will blame this secondary suffering on your ex, even if it was not directly their doing. Although each relationship is unique, others likely are experiencing some of the same pain and anger as you. It's not unusual to harbour anger at your ex, be fearful of the future, or be depressed.

You cannot completely forgive until you've had time to process all the issues. It's even tougher to forgive your ex if he or she continues to be uncooperative; it's worse still if the confrontation continues. As soon as you work through one issue, your ex creates three more. This makes you fearful that if you don't retaliate in some way, your ex will continue this destructive pattern.

At times like these, taking the high road might seem like a weakness, especially when ongoing battling keeps your relational wounds fresh. It is heartbreaking when one or both of you bring the children into your conflict; the children may not understand, and in their own pain, may say or do hurtful things. If you take the high ground, the children will eventually appreciate that you did what you could not to add to the family pain. If this is your situation, dealing with related forgiveness issues becomes easier as your children become adults.

Most people don't understand that it may be necessary to address their need for self-forgiveness for their role in the breakup, as well as to forgive their ex. With painful breakups, there's enough blame to raise self-doubt for years, especially if you tend to dwell on mistakes and wish you'd done things differently. After the breakup, your emotional responses spill over into other areas of your life, including work. When this happens, colleagues may try to give you space, which results in your feeling more isolated. This feeds your self-doubt and reinforces your self-esteem anguish.

You may be able to repress your emotions, at least in the short term. If you tend to compartmentalize your life, your worlds of work and family don't connect. On the outside, all looks fine, as no one at work is aware of what is going on. This makes it easier to ignore. More problems come when you bury problems or deaden your pain in unhealthy ways, such as with prescription drugs or alcohol.

Some people deal with shaken self-esteem by acting out in unaccustomed ways or ending up in relationships more out of neediness than genuine attraction. It happens even for those who know that it's common sense to be wary of rebound relationships. They fear being hurt again, that it won't last, or that the relationship is just wrong. Some people, after a divorce, unconsciously seek out the person who's exactly the opposite of their ex. If you enter into a serious relationship without time to process and address your forgiveness issues, you risk marrying or creating a long-term relationship with the wrong person for the wrong reasons.

There is another possibility when you get into hasty rebound relationships. When you're confused and emotions run wild, and you have unresolved forgiveness, you bring all these issues into your new relationship or marriage. Your new partner is forced to deal with your old problems. This may be part of the reason why the divorce rate for second marriages is higher than for first marriages. It's also why learning the skills to address issues related to a relationship is crucial. The second marriage has a greater chance of success for those who take the time and thereby prevent the ghosts-of-marriage-past from wreaking havoc in the current relationship.

Dealing with All the Changes after Divorce

Many divorced couples face another minefield, as forgiving issues arise with family members and friends. Divorce brings significant change to family celebrations, holiday gatherings, and other social activities. When a husband and wife aren't civil with each other, the entire extended family is affected. They try to figure out ways to keep the peace and how to handle weddings, funerals, and family holidays. The more people involved, the more complicated forgiveness becomes.

If the centre of your married life was shared activities with friends, you may well lose many of those couple friends. They may find it impossible not to take sides; sometimes they feel they're backed into a corner, having to make a choice, thinking they can't socialize the same way with both of you. If you socialized with people your ex works with, being cut off happens almost automatically. You may find all this overwhelming as you become more and more isolated.

When you divorce, you may also inadvertently challenge other couples in dysfunctional relationships who may resent your moving forward or think you have betrayed your marital responsibilities. Others may secretly wish they had the same option. Regardless, your divorce raises issues in their relationship and in their lives.

· It's not as if the impact on everyone ends when your divorce is finalized. If you don't deal with the issues, the tension and anger and lack of forgiveness will sabotage family relationships. There are collateral forgiveness issues, as children tend to blame themselves. For those with a strong religious background, this guilt and pain can be compounded by their religious beliefs. Some divorced people feel ostracized by their church, temple, or other faith community.

Ursula's Story: "The Lone Duck"

For the sake of their children, Ursula and her ex-husband, Tom, decided to live close to each other after their bitter divorce. Ursula and the children stayed in the family home. Tom and his second wife bought a house nearby and became the new couple in the neighbourhood.

Ursula was sad to discover that many of their previous couple friends in the community invited Tom and his new wife to parties, but not her. She felt like the lone duck everywhere she went. She struggled not to become resentful, even though she felt abandoned, and even betrayed, by some of her old friends. She felt not only that her friends were not really her friends after all; she felt judged in the process.

She thought she was over the divorce drama, but she found her anger at Tom intensified, especially as it looked as if he had come through the divorce unscathed and she had lost so much more. Ursula felt secretly ashamed about this and worried that her resentment would spill over to her children.

For Ursula, the many losses she experienced, and her sense of being judged by others, added to her sense of failure. In many ways, she found this more difficult to handle than the marriage breakdown. Her fear, isolation, and increasing anger complicated her forgiveness issues. Fortunately, Ursula had the full support of her family, which helped her work through these issues.

After Divorce: Where to Begin

Use your story about your divorce or your journal to identify your sources of pain and fear. Don't worry if you have difficulty identifying these; it's easier to see other people's issues. This is hard work and there is no quick fix. You may require some help with this work, especially if you're still hurting.

If you thought you had processed your anger, only to discover it again, this doesn't mean you failed. This is part of the process; it means you are called to work at deeper levels towards your own healing and health. To help you move forward, ask questions such as "What is the lesson? What did I learn from the incident that brought all this hurt? What is the silver lining? What, if any, is the gift in being hurt?"

If you feel overwhelmed, work on one issue at a time. Your new knowledge about expectations will help you to avoid being self-critical but at the same time to review objectively your experience, asking: "Were my expectations about the relationship completely off-base? Were there signs I missed that showed the person was not worthy of my trust?"

You're not trying to give up your ability to trust; you're trying to learn from this experience to move forward with your life and enter into life-giving relationships. You may, for example, not jump right in next time, but wait to have others earn your trust over time. This is an invaluable skill. If you are blocked, seek help with this, perhaps with a trusted friend or pastor.

Forgiveness Issues Related to Divorce

Each divorce brings with it different aspects for forgiveness, and each person is affected in their own way. The issues you identified help you sort through areas you may not have identified. It takes time, as even though the couple is legally divorced, that doesn't mean they've divorced emotionally. As we've seen, divorce raises issues including anger, blame, feelings of failure, loss of self-esteem, and self-recrimination. Custody battles raise boundary issues, and sometimes require help from a counsellor. Some divorced people also face issues around doubt, guilt, sin, and questions about God and faith. They may ask: Why did this happen to me? Where is God? Why weren't my prayers answered? Why doesn't my faith community support me? Even when others reach out to help, the divorced people may question their ability to enter fully into their faith community, and may feel betrayed.

Betrayals

There's more than one way for couples to betray each other; these are not always apparent. Identifying them allows you to deal with the betrayal and move on. Whether you realized it at the time or not, when you discover an infidelity, it signifies a turning point in your relationship. Infidelity is a powder keg: it touches so many issues and emotions, including trust, anger, self-esteem, personal security, and pain.

Sometimes, part of the pain of infidelity stems from a serious emotional disconnect, where one person feels shut out by their partner. While infidelity may seem like the end, it doesn't necessarily mean you have to end your relationship. It can be a time to talk about what matters. The end may mark the beginning of significant change. In the best-case scenario, you both use this time to speak your truth and discover more about yourself, each other, and your relationship.

When either person has sex outside the relationship, it changes the relationship in significant ways. The forgiveness issues are never simple, as so many emotions are involved. Some people are puzzled when it appears that others more easily forgive infidelity, or they're in denial. The forgiving spouse believes their partner was not emotionally attached to the other person; they may think, "It was just sex" or "It didn't mean anything." Sometimes infidelity is a symptom of a broader problem, where both individuals bear some responsibility. Regardless, the damage done to the relationship requires hard work from both of them.

Sexual infidelity is not the only form of betrayal. Emotional infidelity happens when one party develops a primary emotional attachment to someone else. The "unfaithful" one has a stronger emotional bond with this third person than with their spouse, even though they remain sexually faithful.

The pain caused by emotional betrayal is often misunderstood or overlooked completely. Current research indicates that for women, emotional betrayal by their partner is as painful as sexual betrayal. Recall Helen's story (Chapter 1), where Helen sought emotional connection with two friends rather than with her husband.

Internet infidelity involves both sexual and emotional infidelity, and the potential for destruction is real. While this is not being unfaithful in the traditional sense, as it's not an in-person relationship, one person in the relationship can end up devoting time and energy to someone else. Research shows dramatic increases in viewing online pornographic sites. Research also indicates that porn is addictive. Most viewers of porn don't think they're being unfaithful, but their partner feels betrayed when they find out. No matter what the betrayal is, forgiving is possible when each partner looks at their relationship, their actions, and what contributed to the situation. They have to work through complex emotions and multiple issues of forgiveness.

Hidden Addictions that Betray

Addicts hurt the ones they love and suck the life out of relationships. There are many forms of addictions and just as many ways for spouses and partners to hurt each other. If one of them is addicted to sex, or gambling, or shopping, it impacts them both. Keeping the addiction secret is another level of betrayal. If your partner lies about their addiction, this damages your relationship, and in many cases, your health and safety as well. Addicts have long lists of betrayals, failed apologies, and requests for forgiveness. The ones who love them feel powerless to understand or help. When this happens, forgiveness feels pointless. If you're the would-be forgiver, you may wonder, "Why bother?" Without addressing the issues, forgiveness feels like weakness, as nothing changes, or it makes things worse.

The danger for the forgiving partner is that forgiving enables the addict's behaviour. If so, the underlying issues are never properly addressed. Over time, the person who is expected to forgive the addict becomes resentful, gets depressed, or gives up.

A Subtle Kind of Betrayal: Undermining Your Spouse

Marriage is a crucible for relationship issues in both positive and negative ways. For some couples, the inability to deal with personal issues hurts both spouses – unemployment, financial difficulties, or in-law challenges distract them from dealing with problems in their relationship. For example, some spouses feel undermined and undervalued when their spouse allows their parents to meddle in their relationship. It's as if their parents take priority. In terms of forgiveness, it's important to find out what actions you want to see happen to address your hurt. Ask your spouse, "Do you understand how I feel when I feel unsupported and undervalued?"

Sadly, sometimes one parent undermines the other as they use their children to manipulate each other (aggressive triangulation – see Chapter 9). Here, one parent makes the other parent out to be the bad guy so they themselves look good. For example, when the mother says, "Wait until your father gets home," she wants to be the good cop. That means the father has to be the bad guy. It is one thing if the couple has decided between them who will provide discipline. It is another if one parent is determined to be the nice one and abdicates disciplinary responsibility, forcing the other parent to relate to the children in a punitive way.

It is also a form of overt undermining when one parent tells the children to be wary of the other parent by saying things like "What will we do if your mother/father finds out?" Children become pawns, drawn into "Let's keep this our little secret."

Many therapists and counsellors now consider it to be abuse when a child witnesses their parents' violent behaviour. Parents who have been abusive with each other forget that children who witness this abuse are also traumatized. Later on, they find they owe their children an apology for their behaviour while their children were growing up.

When Holding Back, or "It's Not You, It's Me," Feels Like Betrayal

What we call commitment avoidance happens when one person withholds their real intentions about what living together means. If the two parties have different assumptions, this causes anguish for one of them. It's important for the couple to discuss their expectations before they move in together or marry. If not, this complicates forgiveness issues, because the two people were operating under different assumptions and expectations (see Chapter 2).

At one of our workshops, a woman shared her experience. She had been married for many years, and even though she longed to have children, she didn't, because her husband didn't want them. Years later, they divorced, as her husband was having an affair with a younger woman. But it was too late, as she put it, as she could no longer have children. For her it was heartbreaking and difficult to forgive, because her ex-husband and new wife eventually had three children.

She realized her anger was not just at her husband and the wasted years satisfying his wishes; she had to deal with her grief at not having a child. Although it was painful for her, she was able to separate the threads of her anger and grief.

For some, the fear is that the commitment avoidant person cares, but not enough to work through difficulties. Ironically, those with the least commitment in a relationship have the most power. This is not necessarily a problem unless one of them uses that power in a way that controls or abuses their partner. In one case, a wife was hypercritical of her husband for years. He endured constant verbal abuse by his wife over this time, for the sake of his children and his commitment to marriage. Eventually, in an irrational outburst, the wife told her husband it would be better for all of them if he left. She expected him to continue his usual pattern of capitulating to her demands and thought he would beg to be able to stay. To her surprise, he chose to break the cycle and leave. He discovered he was happier away from her. Ironically, the wife became increasingly bitter. She laid the blame for his leaving on him, completely negating her role in ending the marriage. As her husband discovered, if you are in a relationship where you are the only one who does all the asking for forgiveness, what does that say about your partner and their ability to be in a healthy relationship?

Working Through Financial Issues

For many couples, the most serious arguments involve money. Forgiveness issues around money are complicated – even more so for relationships, as money issues touch upon your sense of security, self-worth, values, and personal power.

One of the fundamental ways couples depend on each other involves their financial affairs. If you are dealing with financial conflict, pay attention to what this means, as how you spend money reflects your values and beliefs. We all experience anxiety if we feel that our financial security is threatened. Couples must resolve differences in their expectations – for example, about savings plans for education or for retirement.

When there are differences in the couple's financial temperaments, the resulting conflict must be addressed. Sometimes, without realizing it, one or both people try to control the other person through finances (whether they are married/in a relationship or divorced). Be prepared to dig deep to become aware of all the forgiveness complexities related to questions about money. The more you understand money as an emotional issue, social issue, and so on, the more likely it is that you will be able to resolve financial conflicts in your relationship.

Tom's Story: "Should I Tell My Sister?"

When divorce happens, the standard of living is often reduced for everyone involved. These changes potentially foster bitterness and anxiety, as we see in this story:

Tom was worried; he didn't know how to tell his sister Pam what she was doing to her kids after her divorce. Pam constantly complained to her 8-year-old son and 12-year-old daughter that she had no money. Pam complained that she went back to work to make sure the kids didn't have to move and change schools.

Tom wasn't sure of the extent of his sister's financial fears, but he worried that Pam was making her children anxious. He noticed that his niece and nephew worried how much things cost. When their father talked about taking them on a holiday, they wouldn't talk about it with their mom. Tom was pretty sure they thought doing this would be betraying her.

Tom didn't know how to talk to Pam about this. He feared the kids were beginning to confuse money with love for each parent. As Pam was angry and worried, Tom didn't want to add to her worries.

Later, when Tom pointed out to Pam that the kids kept their worries bottled up because they didn't want to trouble either parent, she was completely surprised. When Pam's ex-husband heard about the conversation, he became angry. From his perspective, he had suffered financially and he didn't get to see his children as much as he wanted. This made the situation worse, as he began to express his exasperation in front of their children.

Tom's nephew and niece became increasingly confused, not knowing whose side to take. Eventually, they shut down, not wanting to make things even worse. Tom felt guilty for interfering and couldn't forgive himself. With the best of intentions, he had wanted to help his sister, who did not seem aware of how her comments affected her children. He worried he had crossed a line.

Parents of Divorced Children

The parents of divorcing couples have their own forgiveness issues. Perhaps they feel guilty for having more sympathy for the former spouse than for their own son or daughter. Many grandparents are terrified that divorce will make it difficult to see grandchildren, making it easier to blame. If so, the divorcing parents should talk about options for holidays, grandchildren's visits, and so on. Of course, this presupposes a degree of cooperation among all the parties. Recall Helen's story (Chapter 1), where Helen made a conscious choice to meet with her ex-husband's new wife for the sake of her children.

T/S 16: PRACTISE FORGIVENESS: DEVELOP SKILLS USING SELF-TALK AND ROLE PLAY

Self-talk is a technique that helps you practise saying in a constructive way what you'd like to say to the person who hurt you. Doing this helps you get in touch with your anger or express what you need before you actually speak to the person. It's a safe dress rehearsal.

Self-talk is powerful, when used constructively or unconsciously. You may not realize you're using a form of self-talk when you keep repeating spiteful, angry words that make you angrier. With a trusted friend or therapist, role play also helps with apologies, whether you want to make an apology or receive one. The purpose of role play is to try different scenarios that broaden your perspective and insight. Role play also helps you learn to handle and resolve conflict by giving you insight into the issues you're struggling with.

As you role play, make a point of monitoring your feelings and thoughts. If you find it overwhelming, take a break. Don't worry if you feel stuck or blocked. The feeling of being stuck may be due to your resistance. Resistance may be there for a good reason. Role play helps you deal with resistance in a safe way. As you practise different scenarios, that resistance will likely give way to a deepening awareness of the intricacies of your situation. This could lead to you being able to move forward to a place of healing and forgiving.

12

The Countless Ways Forgiveness Impacts Your Life

The Gifts of Forgiveness

We've seen the benefits or gifts that forgiving brings, including spiritual, mental, and physical well-being. This is why people who forgive often have a sense of calm and peace about them. Forgiving is freeing: it allows us to move forward, make reparations, and bring about healing. For those who experience forgiveness, it can also feel like a gift, even though there are still consequences.

Becoming a forgiving person helps you live an authentic life, as this practice touches on your truth as an individual. You strip away all pretence, self-images, and projections without pumping yourself up or tearing yourself down. This is not always easy; each of us has our own perspective on events, and truth can be painful. Sometimes we're not aware that we're being untruthful. Some memories are so painful and deeply buried that we have no access to them. We avoid painful issues by saying things like "The devil you know is better than the one you don't." We haven't solved the issue; we've settled.

Tensions arise when the other person can't hear what they don't want to hear. Some people avoid any kind of self-reflection that helps put them in touch with truth. Others find truth is too difficult to share. They share only what is safe. While this is understandable, it hampers their ability to forgive because they cannot state their personal truth. They are blocked. Sadly, some people cannot deal with the truth needed for forgiving. They don't want to deal with core issues, as this seems to be a safer way to live, even though they remain paralyzed in hurt and anger.

Although addressing truth can be risky and painful, it is a necessary part of forgiving. The quality of forgiveness depends on the openness of each person and their ability to state their truth, to say how they see the issue. Being truthful depends on their ability to take responsibility for their choices. Deep forgiveness requires self-evaluation (T/S 3).

Even though, as we have seen, forgiving is an internal process – emotional, rational, and spiritual – forgiveness happens as a result of interactions with others. Part of the challenge in forgiving is learning to recognize how we have been hurt. In this chapter, we look at a range of forgiveness issues in the most common areas: with family and friends, at work, and with institutions such as schools, churches, or government. This overview helps you identify these issues so you can apply the Tools and Strategies in your own circumstances. This list is by no means comprehensive, nor is it intended to be.

We turn to Margaret's story. She couldn't get over what happened to her friend Lillian and wanted to find out why saying sorry didn't work and why this situation bothered her so much.

Forgiveness within Families

Margaret's Story: "Why Wasn't My Friend Forgiven?"

Margaret was happy telling everyone how much she enjoyed taking care of her granddaughter during the week while the child's parents were working. She was careful to respect her daughter-in-law's ideas about child rearing, even when she did not agree.

Margaret was unsettled by what happened to her friend Lillian, who also looked after her grandchildren. Lillian let her grandchildren eat chicken nuggets even though this was expressly against the parents' wishes to eat vegan. Even though Lillian regretted her actions, her son told her that daycare space was available and it would be good for the children to go there instead of

Lillian's house. For Lillian, this abrupt change was devastating; she felt the real reason for the change was not spoken. She tried to get friends and other family members to help sort it out, but it only made things worse.

Margaret was relieved to finally understand what it was that bothered her about Lillian's story as we looked at underlying forgiving issues and family interactions. She realized that Lillian didn't really want to find a solution; she wanted to show how badly she had been treated. She wanted her friends and other family members to take her side. Lillian blamed her daughter-in-law for taking revenge for what Lillian thought was a trivial matter.

This story may bring to mind someone you know who keeps talking about a problem again and again. Every time they tell their story, they feel justified. This makes things worse; they become angrier and more bitter each time they tell it. Their compulsion to tell all gives them a false sense of superiority. They're not concerned about the privacy of the other people involved. Their endless retelling of how they've been wronged is a way of getting revenge. It can be covert aggression (see Chapter 7) as they destroy the other person's reputation.

Those with a compulsion to tell their tale of woe suffer as a result; their ability to deal with new hurts is impaired. You may know someone who seemed to handle huge problems only to crash over something trivial. Their anger or pain over unresolved issues may have been overloaded, so anything can be the straw that breaks the camel's back. Sadly, they don't realize the cost of not forgiving and the need to address issues.

Child–Parent Issues

Parents make mistakes; fortunately, most often the parents' love and commitment make up for these. But sometimes their actions harm the children; these situations must be addressed by the parents or with outside help. For example, associations such as Adult Children of Alcoholics (ACOA) help adult children become aware of damaging behaviours so they can address issues stemming back to childhood and make healthy changes.

Sometimes parents pass on dysfunction from their own childhood without realizing it. Sometimes the adult child forgives their parents for undermining or even damaging their life because of the parents' unfair or unrealistic expectations. We spoke with one woman who was bitter that her parents supported her brother's university studies, but not hers. For years, she struggled with her anger, as she wanted to become a doctor. Her parents' expectation was that her brother should be supported as he was a male. Eventually, she realized their decision was based in their cultural expectations, rather than a lack of love.

Sometimes the adult child remains stuck in a child-like relationship with parents. They want to be treated as adults, and at the same time they want support. They continue to act with a "Mom or Dad will fix it" mindset. They want this, yet they resent being bailed out of problems. For relationships that evolve over time, parents and adult children must look at healthy boundary changes. There are challenging issues when parents of adult children harbour resentment over childhood/teen issues long since past, or resent the choices their children make as independent adults, such as career choice, choice of partner, or not practising their faith.

At one of our retreats, a woman complained she had done everything she could to get her son, Eddie, to marry Jocelyn, whom he was living with. It wasn't that she liked Jocelyn, but she thought their relationship was scandalous. The problem was that Eddie avoided his mother, as he resented her interference. He knew his mother placed all the blame on Jocelyn for the situation. It became destructive for all of them, as blaming others makes forgiving nearly impossible.

Death in the Family

During times of stress, unresolved forgiveness issues within the family often play out. When there's a death, the family may not be equipped to deal with the raw emotions that run deep. Some families come together at funerals – this is either a time for forgiveness and reconciliation, or it makes everything worse.

Death brings with it buried forgiveness issues, including unresolved competition for parents' affection. In one story that a client shared, siblings experienced tension when their parents left the bulk of their assets only to their sons, not their daughters. Even though the adult daughters understood that this reflected their parents' traditional cultural values, it was nonetheless hurtful. It made it even harder to work through forgiving issues when the explanation did not make sense to the next generation.

Elder Abuse

Taking care of a parent is a wonderful gift, although the adult child may not feel it at the time. A number of factors contribute to the possibility of elder abuse, which can take many forms, including emotional, physical, or financial abuse. As parent and child age, their relationship changes, and often their roles are reversed and the adult child becomes the caregiver. This involves different levels of struggle: for example, the adult child may struggle with a vague anger at unresolved conflicts, where long-standing issues linger. Sometimes the adult children feel guilty or angry for resenting increased demands, as the parent requires more time and energy. When resources are limited, frustration becomes increasingly difficult to handle. The adult child knows their anger is irrational, but they still feel it. To address their anger in a healthy way, they must acknowledge it and seek outside help if they need it.

Emotional, Physical, Sexual, and Spiritual Abuses of Children

Child abuse is horrendous in all circumstances. Those who were abused as children may not have dealt with or even acknowledged their experience. Ideally, adults recognize that as children they had no control over the incident. But this is where some adult survivors get stuck: they can't forgive themselves for what happened in childhood. In the worst-case scenario, self-recrimination magnifies the damage of the original trauma.

Adults who remain traumatized benefit from professional therapy, particularly when their security was threatened. Therapists help them deal with lack of support when they were children. They do not betray the family when they speak their truth; on the contrary, they give the family an opportunity to deal with the abuse openly for the first time. As long as abuse remains covert (hidden), it won't be dealt with, and it can happen again. In terms of forgiving, healing takes place when people who have been abused do not collude with family secrets or dysfunction. It may take years for family members to deal with the ramifications and their own forgiveness issues about what happened.

Cultural Clashes

Far too often, conflicts arise between people of different cultures due to prejudice and misunderstanding. Conflict stems from cultural blindness, which is often based on lack of information and misunderstanding – false assumptions (see Chapter 2). In terms of forgiveness, wanting to be fair with others is not enough. As part of forgiving, those who have hurt people of another culture must start by learning more about that culture and how this impacted how they hurt them.

Forgiveness Issues for Sexual Minorities

In many parts of the world, people whose sexual orientation is not the norm experience hurts ranging from prejudice to violence. Many feel ostracized as families and friends marginalize them. For example, family members cause pain by dismissive remarks about homosexuality. Often, these issues are not addressed. Sometimes they are addressed at the last possible moment, such as when a parent is dying and wants to make amends with their son or daughter.

Top-down Official Forgiveness

We've seen that forgiving is a process experienced on emotional, psychological, and spiritual levels that takes place within the person who forgives. We usually think of forgiving as being relational, happening between individuals. There are times when it is necessary and just that you receive an apology from someone in authority, such as a company, church, or government. This happens, for example, when you've been hurt by an individual in their role as part of the institution. For you, this person not only represents but is the church, the school, or the university. It is necessary for a person in authority to also address the hurt done by a coach, a priest, or someone in a leadership position.

Official Forgiveness

Sometimes wrongs are committed against everyone who's part of a particular religion, ethnicity, or minority. These situations present special challenges for forgiving. When an entire group has been wronged, the wrongful treatment has to be acknowledged publicly at some point. This may take place decades or even generations later.

When the leader of the offending group or institution conveys an understanding of the issue, this creates a healing environment. It is essential to provide the groundwork for dialogue so that those who've been hurt can speak their truth. They need to tell what happened so that they feel respected and protected. Official government apologies that recognize wrongs, as well as Truth and Reconciliation commissions, help make this possible.

Being on the Receiving End: Official Apologies

As we have seen, forgiveness is personal; no one can forgive on your behalf. If you've been hurt because you're a member of a minority or a particular culture, how do you process an impersonal group apology? If you've been hurt as an individual because of your ethnic background or religion, this hurts as much as if you were harmed for who you are as an individual, and increases the number of layers of forgiveness that need to be addressed.

In 2008, Prime Minister Stephen Harper apologized to Canada's Indigenous peoples for the federal government's role in operating residential schools dating back to the 1870s. In 1993, US President Bill Clinton apologized for the overthrow of the Kingdom of Hawaii in 1893. For some people, these apologies opened up the possibility of addressing historical wrongs by acknowledging their suffering as individuals and as members of a minority. At a fundamental level, public recognition is the first step in truth.

Receiving a Courtroom Apology

Whenever you're involved with a system, you need to know how this affects forgiveness, especially if you want to avoid adding to your pain. When you've been victimized by crime, your involvement with the system complicates forgiving, as the system operates under specific rules and regulations. Once begun, the judicial and legal processes have their own timing and momentum, which may overwhelm you.

You lose privacy when you become involved with a system. It's possible to feel a sense of despair if the outcome you hoped for doesn't happen. The danger is that you may feel worse, even bitter, when you hear an apology from the person convicted of a crime. Even in the best-case scenario, where justice has been served and the offender is convicted, there is no guarantee you will experience a sense of peace or think the sentence was adequate.

Even though sharing victim impact statements can be a positive experience, as victims share their feelings about what happened, recent research suggests this can be counter-productive, as their expectation for justice is not always satisfied. When the victims feel heard (Chapter 3), this is healing. If it feels like a token gesture, they feel revictimized.

It's important to be aware of the strengths and limitations of systems when it comes to forgiving. Increasingly, governments are concerned with forgiveness and reconciliation, as we have seen with the Truth and Reconciliation Commissions in South Africa and Canada. Many have found this process helpful, as they find it restores a sense of power, which is a necessary part of forgiveness.

Nelson Mandela has shared with the world how he was able to forgive after suffering years of imprisonment. Mandela was able to forgive in spite of the actions of others and the decisions made by authorities. His leadership, in so many areas, but especially with regard to forgiveness, is remarkable, considering the pain borne by so many under apartheid.

As we have seen, forgiveness involves being able to speak and listen to truth. Some of those involved in the truth and reconciliation process made conscious decisions to forgive without demanding retribution. Others think they could forgive if the wrong had been corrected and restitution has been made. It is important, especially for those who expect justice, to understand that what you want, and perhaps what you need, will not necessarily be the outcome.

Forgiveness Issues and Institutions

Particular issues emerge when forgiving is connected with an institution such as a church, club, university, or athletic team. Multiple levels of being hurt exist as the victims must deal with the offending person, with the institution's response to what happened, and with family members. Sometimes the victims are not believed, or they're told they are somehow to blame, which adds to the suffering. Other times, they're expected to be silent for the good of the team, the school, or the church. The victim may forgive what happened and choose to remain silent for their own reasons. Ironically, silence harms everyone concerned, including the institution. Being silent leads to cover-ups and no impetus for change.

Many victims feel doubly betrayed by the reaction, or inaction, of institutional leaders after reporting abuse. When the abuse took part in a religious setting and nothing is done, they face multiple levels of loss, including loss of their faith, loss of respect for church leadership, and loss of their place in the church, team, or school.

Contradictory messages about forgiveness cause confusion. When authorities expect victims to remain silent or dutifully forgive, this is a form of revictimization. It takes away accountability. It may appear that authorities are more protective of the abuser than the victim. For the victim, it feels as if the painful event did not matter. For the abuser, being forgiven without accountability can be interpreted as deliverance from responsibility. Forgiveness only happens where the abuse is truthfully dealt with, based in respect (T/S 1) so everyone involved can address the pain and move on.

13

Forgiveness: Religion and Spirituality

I n this chapter, we focus on the religious and spiritual perspectives about forgiveness, as the religious dimension adds depth to understanding the forgiveness process. We make a distinction between religion and spirituality even though for many, the terms are interchangeable; others see themselves as being spiritual, but not religious. We look at what moves you beyond revenge, anger, and bitterness to a conscious, intentional life. We also look at possible ways religion and spirituality hinder forgiveness. We suggest ways to deepen forgiving as part of your spiritual practice and ways to help you practise your faith, both of which help you become more in touch with the benefits of forgiving.

For our purpose here, we talk about religion in the sense that it provides a cohesive framework for understanding and for living. Religions also provide a sense of community: believers gather to worship and do good works, such as by serving those in need. For those who look, religious beliefs can provide the groundwork for all relationships: with one another, with the Creator, and with creation. Faith can help individuals become more compassionate, more forgiving. Religion helps with questions such as these: Is God always forgiving? Can forgiveness be freely given, or must it be earned? Are we somehow hardwired to seek revenge, or do we have choice?

Working to achieve forgiveness is part of many religious and spiritual practices. Many religions, including Christianity, Judaism, Islam,

Buddhism, and the writings of Confucius share a form of the Golden Rule: for example, the Bible tells us, "Do to others what you would have them do to you," while the Qur'an says, "Not one of you is a believer until he loves for his brother what he loves for himself. So in everything, do to others what you would have them do to you, this sums up the Law and the Prophets."

As an adult, it is enlightening to re-examine your beliefs about forgiving, especially if you have not really looked at these since you were a child. While it is not possible here to look in depth at forgiveness within all the major religious traditions, we invite you to seek out the wisdom within your faith or one you feel drawn to at this stage in your life. The best advice is to avoid making assumptions rooted in a childhood understanding. Consider finding a group or someone to journey with you as you explore. We encourage you now, with your new-found skills and knowledge, to look at all the ways your religion helps you bring about forgiveness: for example, by participating in Penitential services in Lent and Advent, the Day of Atonement, or other spiritual forgiving practices. You also have the Tools and Strategies in this book to help you process forgiveness – by placing them in the context of your religion, you can deepen your forgiving and your faith.

Don's Story: "Forgive or Suck It Up?"

Don shared his struggle with the idea of having to forgive without compromising his workplace integrity and values, which are very important to him in his Lutheran faith.

I was quite new at the company. At first it didn't bother me, but I got tired of being given the work assignments no one wanted. Worse yet, the work I did went unrecognized. I did my best no matter what, hoping things would change. It was the last straw when my boss took the credit, and a bonus, for a project I'd done. I didn't know what to do: say nothing, and suck it up yet again? Or look for another job?

My faith tells me to forgive, but this was a struggle. The trouble was, this had happened to me before – my boss said that next time, my work would be acknowledged. He said there were lots more opportunities for bonuses. It was hard to accept his explanation and what he thought was an apology. I'm a forgiving person, but I did not want to be taken advantage of again.

At first, Don felt compelled to forgive again, even though the issues had never been addressed. The more Don learned about the complexity and the process of forgiving, the more comfortable he was. He no longer stressed about living his values as a man of faith at work. Don requested a meeting so he and his boss could talk about the situation in a professional manner. Don wanted to be absolutely clear about his expectations (his boundaries). Having a greater understanding of forgiving that you can forgive and expect changes empowered him to take the necessary steps, which clarified the issue for both Don and his boss. His clarity about what forgiving means also helped him prevent others from taking advantage of him.

Christian Forgiveness

As we said in the introduction, for Christians, Christ is the model, not just for living forgiveness, but for life. We cannot overemphasize the significance of the gift of forgiveness for Christ's followers – in his life, teachings, words, and actions. Forgiveness was so important to him that when followers asked him how they should pray, he instructed them to pray daily, to "forgive others as you have been forgiven." When asked, Christ told others to forgive not once, but "seven times seventy" times! He forgave even with his last breath. Forgiveness is part of the bedrock of his teachings and of Christian faith.

As we've seen, those who make a choice to forgive and address the issues with truth foster complete forgiving. Some people hinder their forgiving when they think mainly in terms of the duty to forgive. They feel guilty when they cannot fulfill this obligation, thinking there's something wrong with them, or they're not faithful enough. People of faith help their forgiving the more they understand forgiving as being done out of love, and by choice as followers of Christ. When viewed this way, forgiveness is a life-giving spiritual practice rather than merely a duty or a burden. When you honour your faith and allow yourself choice, you allow yourself to be open. When you are open, the Spirit works in you.

The Sacrament of Reconciliation

Forgiveness is a critical part of healthy relationships in all faith traditions. Many faith traditions set times and rituals for communal forgiveness, recognizing that fractured relationships negatively impact the community and personal spiritual growth. Roman Catholics seek forgiveness in celebrating the sacrament of reconciliation. This sacrament emphasizes the need for forgiveness and one's longing for one's relationship with God and with others to be restored.

In the early Church, the person seeking reconciliation was required to confess their sins before the whole community and to do penance for a long period, such as up to a year. Today, the sacrament of reconciliation is experienced privately, between the priest (representing Christ and the community of faith) and the person confessing their sins. For believers, this sacrament is a profound experience. It brings Christ's forgiveness to life: the penitent hears the words "You are forgiven" from a priest who listens as they speak their truth (see T/S 9).

During a special Year of Mercy (2015–2016), Pope Francis encouraged all the Catholic faithful to respond to the call for forgiveness and reconciliation. He longed to share the good news that forgiveness is a gift from God, and this sacrament heals the heart and soul.

For those who experience the sacrament of reconciliation, the more forgiving they become, the more they deepen their experience of God. Sometimes those who don't understand the sacrament are critical, thinking that some people use it as a "Get out of jail free" card. In one sense it can be! This is the radical nature of the sacrament: God's willingness to freely forgive and reconcile is absolute. While it is possible that someone could misunderstand or misuse the sacrament, who would do so, knowing they're missing a crucial opportunity to deepen their relationship with God?

If you are Catholic and want to deepen your openness and healing through the sacrament of reconciliation, we urge you to take time to prepare by praying and reflecting on your actions – what you've done and what you've failed to do – that harmed yourself and others. Ask yourself: Why do you see it as a sin rather than simply breaking a rule? What relationship has been harmed? What do you wish you had done differently? Why are you going to celebrate this sacrament? What are you feeling? Focus on the experience and what it means to be forgiven.

Helping and Hindering Forgiveness

The Shadow Side: When Believers' Duty Thwarts Forgiving

Bishop Geoffrey Robinson of Australia spent years working with cases of sexual abuse by clergy. He says that in some cases, the Church manipulated victims for its own purposes to avoid scandal. This reflects the shadow side of religious obligation, where individuals are told it's their duty to forgive the abuser. However, the victim's anger at their Church and possibly at religion in general must be affirmed as a valid response to the abuse. When knowledge of wrongdoing is suppressed, problems remain under cover and more individuals can be victimized. Justice cannot take place under cover; it needs the light of day.

Spiritual Practices for Forgiving

Here, spirituality includes different religious traditions, as well as Indigenous spiritualities, and contemporary ones, such as eco-spirituality. Those who engage in a spiritual practice reflect a desire to be open to growth as a human being. It also includes those who seek a connection with the "Sacred Other."

Briefly, for our purposes here, spirituality is soul work. We focus on your thoughts, words, and actions (the way you live your life), as well as those practices that reflect your core values and your relationships. Forgiving is an essential part of soul work, as it affects your relationship with others and with the divine. Part of this soul work is developing compassion and humility. The more you deepen your practice of forgiving, the more you get in touch with your woundedness: hurts you have received and have caused.

When you engage in forgiveness as a spiritual practice, you are invited to remove blinders, to wake up and see. In other words, you withdraw your projections (Chapter 2). Those who practise forgiveness with a spiritual focus bring it to life through meditation and prayer, and right action with others. As you deepen your spiritual practice, your healing deepens as well. This is a gift of forgiving.

With spirituality as our focus, we suggest practices and new ways of envisioning forgiveness to assist you to a place of openness and inspiration. Alter these practices to suit your own circumstances and in accordance with your spiritual life. As with most spiritual practices, these require time and commitment. If appropriate, consider joining a group for support, inspiration, and guidance – such as a group that meets for prayer (centering prayer, meditation).

Forgiveness and the Divine

Centuries after the poet Alexander Pope wrote, "To err is human, to forgive, divine," it still makes sense whether we are religious or not. Some would say that forgiving has to be divine because it goes against a biological imperative. We're hardwired to seek revenge. At times, forgiving seems impossible. It makes no sense; it defies logic; the only explanation is that a higher power is involved.

Living Forgiveness

Forgiveness work is soul transforming; this deep-rooted inner peace is evident in teachers and practitioners in various spiritual practices. Great spiritual teachers seek compassion, wisdom, and peace. As they work to embody charity and mercy, they are transformed, becoming living forgiveness. Forgiving becomes integral to them, so that they no longer think of forgiveness as an ideal; forgiving is their way of living. They help form a bedrock for peace building in the world.

This kind of living forgiveness doesn't preclude sorrow or prevent suffering, but it can't easily be taken away, even under extreme circumstances, such as imprisonment, punishment, or even death. This peace is based in truth; it doesn't mean those who forgive ignore, cover up, forget, or repress what happened. Forgiving gives them the strength to let go and move on in their life. It also gives them wisdom and strength to help others.

When a person who embodies living forgiveness seeks forgiveness, they focus on the other person's welfare, unlike the person who seeks forgiveness for their own relief, or to make things go away. Those who embrace living forgiveness don't push forward; they respect when the other person isn't ready to forgive. The point is not to cause the other more pain in an effort to make amends and be forgiven.

In some cases, the one who aspires to living forgiveness makes amends quietly, so that no one else knows about it. In the story of *Les Misérables*, Jean Valjean steals silverware from a priest who had given him food and a place to stay. Later, Jean was caught and brought back to the priest's house by the police. The priest showed mercy and compassion by telling the police that he had given Jean the silver. This experience of living forgiveness helped Jean turn his life around. He became merciful and compassionate, spending his life as living forgiveness as well. As we see in the story of Jean Valjean, the more forgiveness you experience, the more you are able to give away.

You may know someone or have heard stories about those who say that without their faith, they could not forgive. Their faith not only encouraged them, it made forgiving possible.

Janet's Story: "A Lifetime of Grief"

Janet was 70 years old. She explained that when she was a young mother, one of her three pre-school-age daughters managed to get into the medicine cabinet and died after taking some pills.

She went on to say, "Death visited me again 40 years later"; when another daughter was brutally murdered by her husband, Janet's friends and family rallied around to help.

No one, especially her surviving daughter, could believe it when Janet said she forgave her son-in-law. Some were angry; others accused her of being disloyal to her murdered daughter. Some saw her forgiveness as a betrayal of their support and friendship. The fact that Janet was able to come to a place of peace confused her friends and family.

In the aftermath of her daughter's murder, Janet had to deal with her grief as well as the anger of those who did not want her to forgive. Yet she forgave in spite of criticism and pressure from others. She was not able to say *how* she was able to forgive, only that she did. She was thankful, saying her faith helped her. She wanted to share her story to help others understand. Janet's faith and her ability to forgive allowed her to move forward so she was not stuck in grief, despair, or anger. By forgiving, she was also able to remember and be thankful for her wonderful daughter.

Developing a Forgiveness Stance

Forgiving is not always easy. For most people, even with the best intentions, forgiving must be intentionally nurtured. You do this, for example, by consciously and intentionally developing a forgiveness stance. As you do this, you integrate forgiving to such an extent that it becomes second nature – you forgive because it is who you are. Martin Luther King understood this. He said, "Forgiveness is not an occasional act. It is a permanent attitude." Those who develop their forgiveness stance become a healing presence in the world. Those who focus on spirituality may see developing their forgiveness stance in terms of being in harmony with the divine. Many of the world's great spiritual leaders help us see forgiving as living out of our deepest, truest selves.

Forgiving Receptivity

By seeking forgiving receptivity, you open yourself to the kind of knowing that is accessible through prayer and meditation as well as learning skills and educating yourself. This means accepting the human condition, with all its limitations, including your own. You acknowledge the truth: the truth of the other person, the truth of the situation, and your own truth. When you are in touch with your own experience of being forgiven, it is easier to forgive others.

A spirit of receptivity means doing all you can to withdraw your projections, to withdraw your own set of expectations and assumptions of someone else (see Chapter 2). It means not only respecting them (T/S 1) but honouring the light within them. You recognize that the other person is different and has their own path in life.

Being open to finding out that the person who hurt us was also hurt in the past sometimes helps us see how they hurt us in a different light. For example, they may have come from an abusive family, or suffer from post-traumatic stress disorder. Their experience doesn't give them the right to hurt others, but this knowledge of this past may help you sort out all the issues and act with this knowledge. If they are open, you may help the other person so they change hurtful behaviours. With a spirit of forgiving receptivity, you help provide a healing environment.

Seeking Truth

In terms of spirituality, forgiveness acknowledges the truth of who we are as individuals. When you see yourself for who you truly are, you strip away all pretenses and self-images, and withdraw projections. Forgiveness is also truth in that it brings you closer to the person you were created to be. This kind of truth refers to your self rather than your ego. Another way of saying this is to see the difference between your true self and your false ego. You hear this echoed in the writing of Teresa of Avila, Thomas Merton, and Thomas Keating.

A young woman once asked us if confession (the sacrament of reconciliation) could be misused. She wondered if Catholics could avoid responsibility for their behaviour by choosing this action. While it is possible for someone to confess without taking responsibility or wanting to making restitution, that person would not have been seeking truth.

Spiritual Traps

Certain attitudes hinder forgiving. One is being overly scrupulous: self-critical to the point that you harshly judge everything you do, which contributes to inappropriate guilt. It is all-or-nothing thinking: you are good or bad; right or wrong. This overemphasis on errors, personal weakness, and failures leads a person to spend their energy on avoiding the bad rather than striving for the good.

Such a person's negative self-image reinforces their view that the world is unforgiving, and they fear that God is unforgiving. They feel guilty, as they can't live up to their impossible standards. They apologize when it is unnecessary, as no offense occurred except in their minds. If you suffer from scrupulosity, seek out a therapist who specializes in this issue, or find a knowledgeable spiritual director.

We Are "One" in Our Search for Forgiveness

Being aware of your need for forgiveness creates a mindset that helps you to forgive those who seek your forgiveness. We all need to forgive as much as we need forgiveness. In childhood, the dynamics may be "Since you hit me, I hit you." This thinking includes the idea of payback and "might is right." As we mature, we need to move beyond this limited view of "an eye for an eye," recognizing that each of us is capable of wounding and being wounded. We help bring about peace as we recognize "we are one" in our need for each other for forgiveness.

Forgiving When the Other Person Doesn't Know They Hurt You

How do you forgive comments that make you feel worse when things are already bad? We all know how hard it is to offer words of comfort in tragic circumstances. At certain times, such as the death of a loved one, well-meaning people can add to your pain. Knowing that such comments are often rooted in their own anxiety about pain may help you forgive them.

In life, when you experience a shattering loss, such as the death of a child, it's understandable to be angry, even with God. It hurts when someone says something like "Your child is better off now, with the angels" or "They'll never grow old." This sets up a disconnect between their comments and your feelings, which adds to your anguish.

It feels entirely different when someone acknowledges your pain, saying, "I'm so sorry for your loss." This person is letting you know that they recognize your pain.

Handling Anger at God

For people of faith, it can be confusing: how can they forgive if they're angry with God when bad things happen, especially if they think, "I do all the right things. I pray. I go to church," and so on. It helps to remember that people get angry even with people they love dearly, and relationships survive. God can handle your anger.

The fact that you're angry with God reflects the fact that God matters in your life. Even though it takes courage to ask, "Why is this happening to me?" it's more helpful to look at your expectations about what should happen (see Chapter 2). Asking why bad things happen is quite different from expecting, or demanding, that bad things should not happen to good people.

Humility and Forgiveness

Even though humility is an important aspect in forgiving, it's often misunderstood. It's easy to confuse behaviours that mimic humility with actual humility, and this confuses forgiving. A person who lacks self-esteem may appear to be humble, as they constantly apologize and are always taking the blame. People lacking self-esteem find it hard to express their real feelings, or what matters (recall that forgiveness requires truth). Humble people are comfortable with truth; they're comfortable taking compliments as well as accepting criticism. They're thankful for God-given gifts; they do not act from an ego-centred pride.

Those who are genuinely humble also recognize others' contributions to their success. Those with humility are free to forgive and be forgiven based in truth and respect.

Work with a Trusted Companion or Spiritual Guide

Find a trusted person, a companion who can walk with you on your spiritual journey to help you with issues of forgiveness. They will hold up a mirror to you, telling you respectfully what they see and what you need to hear (T/S 3). Ask someone who is not likely to reinforce your weaknesses. Friends, understandably, are supportive, but having support and comfort doesn't necessarily lead to growth. We grow when we are challenged, as we wrestle with decisions about what we need to do as opposed to what we would like to do.

A spiritual guide will challenge you to look at your options and see other perspectives so you can take the high road. They will point you towards developing your forgiveness stance and receptivity and help you deepen your forgiveness practice.

14

Radical Forgiving
and Ultimate Freedom

If you feel that you've done all that you can – you've learned about forgiving and tried the Tools and Strategies to bring about forgiveness in your life – there's more! If you want to become ultimately free, the next step is to become what we call "a healer with scars." You bring this teaching to life by including it in your meditation, prayer, or spiritual practice, and by choosing mindful forgiving actions. Radical forgiving is a cornerstone; your focus may be on building peace, following in the footsteps of Christ, or following other spiritual leaders. One of the greatest gifts you bring is living with integrity. Those who provide leadership through their words and their actions as forgiving people are peace builders.

Build an Enduring Legacy: A Forgiveness Print

Forgiveness is more than an ideal to strive for; forgiving is part of your legacy. Your legacy is not just things you accumulate; it is built as a result of your words and deeds, which live on in people whose lives you touch. This is your "forgiveness print." Throughout your life, what seems like a trivial action has a significant impact on others. As you forgive, your actions, like the butterfly effect, create ripples that spread far and wide. There are exceptional individuals whose forgiveness print is passed on from generation to generation. We all benefit from spiritual leaders such as Gandhi, Nelson Mandela, Martin Luther King,

St. Francis of Assisi, and Jesus, whose life and words gave the world enduring forgiveness prints.

Forgiving Presence

Your forgiveness presence is your ability to communicate that you have forgiven in non-verbal ways, which are not always obvious, as we saw in the story of Jean Valjean and the way the priest demonstrates forgiveness. Gary's story also helps us get a glimpse of forgiveness presence. Gary loaned his brand-new car to Hank, his younger brother. Lending it was a big deal for Gary, as it had taken him years to save for his dream car. Gary talked to Hank to make sure he would drive carefully, including parking away from other cars.

When Hank brought the car back, it was obvious that he felt awful about the dent. Gary didn't yell; he calmly asked what happened. To Hank's relief, Gary suggested ways he could pay to repair the car. Nothing more was said, but they both knew the issue was resolved when later, Gary joked with his brother about his parking skills.

Gary never said he forgave his brother; his presence and sensitive response spoke louder than words. Gary listened to his brother calmly. He didn't yell or punch a wall. They both knew that what happened, happened; they agreed on how to fix the problem, and when the car was fixed, the issue was over. Knowing this provided closure for both brothers. The fact that Gary joked about it made them both feel comfortable. This indicated to both of them that all was forgiven, and they moved on.

From Wounded Healer to Healer with Scars

The idea of a wounded healer has inspired humankind since antiquity; the Greek physician Asclepius provided a place for others to heal based on his experience. Many centuries later, the founder of analytical therapy, Carl Jung, offered insights about the need for psychiatrists and therapists to become conscious of their own emotional trauma in order to help clients. Later, Henri Nouwen, a renowned author and spiritual leader, shared his life experience as a model to show others how his woundedness enabled him to love and help others.

Today, the knowledge that wounded healers provide benefits is an integral aspect in many fields, including therapy, spiritual direction, and counselling. Current medical and therapeutic practices recognize former addicts as some of the best addiction counsellors. They are acutely aware of the pitfalls. Those they counsel experience acceptance rather than feeling judged. These wounded healers can require those who seek healing to do difficult tasks, because they have undergone the same experience themselves. Wounded healers give hope to those who worry that they will never regain a normal life.

When it comes to the deep nature of healing that comes with forgiving, there is another level that we call a "healer with scars." Even though these kinds of scars are not visible, they represent a person's surviving a traumatic experience, and show they have healed. For that reason, these scars are valued. They offer hope for others; a healer with scars is a healing presence and a forgiving presence. The shift from being a wounded healer to a scarred healer is a subtle but important paradigm shift. Being a healer with scars is not a matter of strength or pride; it is often based in faith or spirituality, where their compassion shows through.

Just as those who are wounded are not all healers, being scarred does not mean they are a healer. It is possible to become a scarred victim. With emotional trauma we say things like "They were scarred for life." For healers with scars, being scarred means the painful event is now part of their history. It does not define them; they are no longer victims. A healer with scars is someone who has gained wisdom, someone others go to for advice.

Both the wounded healer and the healer with scars use their experience to help others. In terms of forgiveness, being aware of your ability to hurt others allows you to see yourself in the person who hurt you. Even though we recognize how beneficial the notion of a wounded healer is, we invite you to envision yourself becoming a healer with scars, offering your experience as a way to help others. Because the healer with scars feels their wound has healed, they do not need to self-protect the way a wounded person might. In terms of forgiveness, a healer with scars doesn't say, "I can't go there; it's too painful," but "I've been there. I may be able to help."

Envisioning yourself as a healer with scars reduces the risk of identifying as a victim and with how you have been hurt. Because healers with scars have worked through the relevant issues and moved away from victimhood, they do not attract victims.

A living forgiveness person also thinks in terms of being a healer with scars, a person whose wound has healed and now serves them. A healer with scars is able to use their experience to help others overcome difficult situations – to speak their truth, even when it is painful, as we saw in Maria's and Janet's stories (Chapters 10 and 13).

Life-changing and Life-giving Forgiveness

Choosing forgiveness as a way of life and developing a forgiveness stance is one of the more radical choices you can make. It is counter-cultural. We encourage you to trust yourself. It takes courage to live your life based on forgiveness. You will discover the freedom that comes from letting go of painful baggage. You will feel lighter as you address the grudges and hurts. Painful issues no longer have power over you.

Forgiveness is life-giving to you and those you encounter in obvious ways and in ways you can't see. We saw that medical studies show how forgiveness reduces stress. Forgiveness also helps medical conditions such as hypertension, depression, and addiction. By doing forgiveness work, by looking at your assumptions, expectations, and projections onto others, you are better able to unpack the impact of painful events. This can be a turning point, where the choice you make changes your life.

It is understandable that many people feel overwhelmed by the lack of forgiveness in the world. You may ask, "What can one person do?" Until you come to the point of choosing a forgiveness stance, the Tools and Strategies we offer are helpful techniques rather than an integrated lifestyle. They become keys to living when they become second nature. Your forgiving mindset strengthens your forgiveness stance.

Living forgiveness means living life as it actually is, not as you think it should be or as you would like it to be. A forgiveness mindset involves self-revelation, where you speak your truth. Self-revelation can be threatening, leaving you vulnerable to being hurt; paradoxically, it also opens you to growth. By expressing the truth of who you are, you enable others to express their truth as well. We all become healthier whenever someone has the courage to live in accordance with truth.

Forgiveness is essential in transforming your own life and the lives of others. Working for justice becomes more essential the more in touch you become with pain and suffering caused by brokenness. We have seen how revenge magnifies negativity in your life and passes on to others. Richard Rohr, founder of the Center for Action and Contemplation, asks, "Do you transform your pain or transmit it to others?" He suggests that if we do not transform our pain, we will pass it on, even to loved ones, including the next generation. When we forgive, the negativity stops.

World leaders such as Nelson Mandela, Gandhi, and other writers and activists cannot bring about peace on their own. Each and every individual's forgiveness print adds to the sum total of peace building in the world. Those with a spiritual focus understand that "Blessed are the peacemakers" means each person's contributions make a difference. Each person's mindful forgiveness actions contribute to joint efforts for global peace. World leaders can inspire and point others in the right direction, but they must not be alone in striving for peace. Those who live believing there is nothing they can do deny their own power. As we've seen, the smallest acts of forgiveness have the power to change lives.

From our own experience and from working with others, we realize that the only way peace will come is when more and more people seek to become living forgiveness. Peace will come when forgiveness becomes a way of life – a forgiveness mindset for each one of us. Justice and mercy are foundations for the world; developing a forgiveness stance, embracing living forgiveness, or becoming a healer with scars are the best choices for lasting peace.

Living Forgiveness, Embracing Peace

Martin Luther King said, "Darkness cannot drive out darkness; only light can do that. Hate cannot drive out hate; only love can do that." We say that revenge cannot drive out revenge; only peace can do that. Anger cannot drive out anger; only peace can do that. Bitterness cannot drive out bitterness; only peace can do that. Embracing forgiveness brings peace.

We have seen how bringing peace into your life begins with you. Sometimes forgiving begins with a small act of kindness or compassion that turns a life around. Each act of forgiving helps brings about peace. Knowing the astonishing power of forgiveness, it makes no sense to hold on to grudges and hurts. Your forgiving impacts others in ways you may never know or understand, like ripples in a pond. When you forgive, you change your relationships, and in turn, these renewed relationships help build community. We are all connected. Healthy communities help create healthy countries, and so on, until we have a healthy world.

ACKNOWLEDGEMENTS

We would like to acknowledge many others who inspired our work and provided valuable insights. We are grateful to Andrew Ortony and Terence Turner for their research on emotions; Carl Jung and Henri Nouwen for insights on the wounded healer; Murray Bowen for differentiation and triangulation; Martin Seligman for learned helplessness; Albert Bandura for self-efficacy; Edward Lorenz for the butterfly effect; René Girard for scapegoating; Richard Rohr, OFM, for insights on transmitting pain; and Bishop Geoffrey Robinson for work on sexual abuse.

We are grateful for the wisdom and insight in the works of Teresa of Avila, Thomas Merton, and Thomas Keating, Victor Hugo, the Dalai Lama, Nelson Mandela, and Archbishop Desmond Tutu. We are thankful to Martin Luther King, Pope John Paul II, and Pope Francis for their example and their teachings on forgiveness.

TOOLS AND STRATEGIES

MARQUIS

Québec, Canada

RECYCLÉ
Papier fait à partir
de matériaux recyclés
FSC® C103567

PERMANENT   100%   BIO GAZ   Garant
                     ÉNERGIE   des forêts
                                intactes